I0438511

I

Love

Horses

and

Tractors

I Love Horses and Tractors

Stories and adventures from a city girl becoming a country girl

JO ANN SALNESS BYARS

FOREWORD BY TERRY GILES

authorHOUSE®

AuthorHouse™
1663 Liberty Drive
Bloomington, IN 47403
www.authorhouse.com
Phone: 1-800-839-8640

© 2011 by Jo Ann Salness Byars. All rights reserved.

No part of this book may be reproduced, stored in a retrieval system, or transmitted by any means without the written permission of the author.

First published by AuthorHouse   06/10/2011

ISBN: 978-1-4634-2487-9 (sc)
ISBN: 978-1-4634-2486-2 (ebk)

Library of Congress Control Number: 2011910052

Printed in the United States of America

Any people depicted in stock imagery provided by Thinkstock are models, and such images are being used for illustrative purposes only.
Certain stock imagery © Thinkstock.

This book is printed on acid-free paper.

Because of the dynamic nature of the Internet, any web addresses or links contained in this book may have changed since publication and may no longer be valid. The views expressed in this work are solely those of the author and do not necessarily reflect the views of the publisher, and the publisher hereby disclaims any responsibility for them.

Dedication

For Kit because she is a ray of sunshine in my life.

For Jane because she emails me every day, keeps me in touch with the real world and is my biggest fan. She is always so supportive of everything I do.

For Steve because he never seems to tire of my Honey Do List and is so good to me and remains the man of my dreams.

For Terry because he has remained my best friend for my entire adult life and has been instrumental in almost every memorable moment of my life since I met him. Thank you.

Foreword

Friendship is an interesting thing. You never know where or when it will strike. If anyone was to know Jo Byars and myself they would probably not understand what we have in common, which would normally be a linchpin to forming a friendship.

To paraphrase the Osmond's, "Jo is a little bit country and I am a little bit rock and roll". The lives we selected for ourselves are worlds apart and provide little or no overlap. Yet, our 40 year friendship is unwavering and unconditional.

Despite outward appearances, for me at least, I fully understand why she is my friend. Jo is one of the purest, most honest, big hearted persons I have ever encountered. I live in a world of negotiation and gamesmanship. Jo is a breath of fresh air. As her book reveals, she is at home with the earth and all of its creatures. She is genuine and authentic. I believe God is in all of us—it just shows up more in Jo.

What makes this remarkable human being even more special is the kindness and sweetness she brings to everything in her life. The reader of her story needs to understand that she is real and what she writes is unmolested by pretense, ego, or self consciousness. It is simply Jo—bringing her own form of beauty to her world.

It makes me proud to know Jo Byars. She reminds me of all those great quotes about how we are supposed to live life. There is, however, one caveat—and it is a big one. Have you heard the saying about how "we should dance as if no one is watching"? Well, believe me—you do not ever want to see Jo dance. But then, that is a whole other story!

Terry Giles

Contents

Chapter 1

THE CAST OF CHARACTERS

*M*e. I am a retired school teacher and coach. I taught Mathematics, Physical Education, Health and coached volleyball and swimming for thirty-four years. All my life I wanted a horse but we lived in the city and I just never got one. When I was very young I used to ride a broomstick with pretend bridle and make trails around the lot next to ours. I also "saddled up" this section of the wall and practiced jumping onto it to ride when I was young. I went for trail rides on rental horses. Steve and I went to a dude ranch several times and we would ride for four hours a day. Horses have always been my passion. I used to be an athlete with my favorite sports swimming and volleyball. My boys' volleyball players used to tell me I had a two credit card vertical—cards lying flat. Now, I am just old but working pretty hard and learning a lot at this farming adventure.

Steve is my husband. He is a Texas farm boy and used to ride bulls. He served twenty-two years in the United States Marine Corps. He is six foot four, strong, very smart and can do just about anything. He is self-taught on almost any subject. He reads five books a week, mostly science fiction and action but also any book or magazine he needs to research something we are working on at the moment. He loves wood working and mechanical things. If we are trying to build something or create something he looks it up and studies how to build it. He is self taught on the computer and if he does not know how to do something he reads the computer book and figures it out. Amazing.

Brian and Janie are our closest neighbors and friends. If Steve has to talk about some project he discusses it with Brian and they figure it out. Brian and Janie built the most incredible house by themselves. It is a perfect house with tile floors, glass fire places, Jacuzzi bath tubs and a vacuum system for the whole house which is just perfect and gorgeous. We frequently have dinner with them and spend a lot of time discussing how to build things or take care of the forest. Janie taught me how to make the best bread and rolls and Brian taught me how to make incredible roasts, gravy and other wonderful meals. Brian gave us the idea and the information and even helped us put in our water vault. They also let us have the hay from their forty acre field of hay for our horses and cattle. They are delightful people.

Tom and Donna are the neighbors who raise cattle. They have been in the cattle or dairy business for thirty-one years. They know a lot about cattle and are willing to share, help, advise but push us to do things ourselves. They have cattle, sheep, goats, llamas, alpacas, dogs and chickens and sometimes turkeys. I can honestly say they have taught us just about everything we know about cattle. They took us to the auction and helped us get our first cattle. They came and helped us when White Face needed help delivering Licorice. They cut and baled Brian and Janie's field for us and did not ask for money. They know where to get good deals on hay and when to buy and sell cattle. They are definitely our role models for country people. Donna bottle feeds goats and calves. She spins her own yarn, knits incredible things and even wins at the local fairs. They are kind, thoughtful and take care of a lot of people in this valley. Tom and Donna are the kind of people that are the back bone of this country. They are hard working, caring, helpful people and they contribute daily to help feed this country. There is always a group of people at their home. People just stop by to chat, share stories, help, offer advice and just enjoy their company.

Garrett and Maralyse are the leaders of the valley as far as I am concerned. They know everyone, they help everyone and they are delightful people. Garrett has more stories and knows so much about everything. He used to be an airline pilot. They are kind, they share and they do so many nice things for people that need help. We always enjoy their company. Garrett will just drive around in his tractor with his snow blower and clean off roads and driveways for people. He once saw a neighbor that had a huge tree cut down in their yard and he brought his chainsaw and log splitter to cut and split it while they were at work. He likes to do anonymous good deeds. He also likes to make me laugh and he is so good with his stories. Maralyse goes out of her way to help people that are sick, lost a spouse or loved one, need help because the river overflowed and washed away everything they had and is just a genuinely good person and fun to talk to and share stories with.

Josh and Joe are two of the neighborhood young men that have put up most of the fences in our whole little valley. They are brothers in their early twenties. They are both over six feet tall, strong, good looking young men and really great workers. They are happy, fun to work with and the absolute best at any task we put them to working on. They both play basketball and like to work on the farms. When we put up our cattle fence they pounded in hundreds of t-posts, pulled four strands of barbed wire for each fence and where we put in corner posts they finished the holes for the posts and tamped them into the ground. They also trimmed and took down small trees and brush and stacked it. I did not think I was old until I watched these delightful working machines with wonderful personalities. Josh and Joe are truly some of the finest young men I have met. This world is a much better place because they are here. They are also in great demand and all the old guys like us could keep them busy forever. We always feel fortunate when they have time to work for us. Josh even does house sitting so that people can get away for a few days. It takes a special person to house sit a farm and be able to do all the things we have going on around here. He feeds cattle, horses, chickens, cat and walks and feeds dogs several times a day. Josh and Joe are a huge and necessary part of this valley.

Donald and Katie. Donald is an old student and volleyball player of mine. He is an excellent volleyball player and one of the nicest people I have ever met. His wife Katie is beautiful, fun, has a great laugh and she is a very hard worker. They are both athletic and do many outdoor activities.

My Siblings: Ty is my oldest brother and he is a doctor. He played football at USC on a full scholarship. Ty's wife Kris is extremely helpful. She does not say much but she gets up early and weeds my garden or plants trees or cleans and loves the animals. Kym is my middle brother and also a doctor. Kym plays guitar, rides the horses and has done a lot of work around this place. Kit is my only sister, a teacher and she is truly a ray of sunshine. Kit was on the Olympic diving team in 1980, the year the US did not go to the Olympics. Lad is my youngest brother and he is a teacher and a coach. He is one of the best coaches I have ever seen. He coaches football, basketball and volleyball. He was just named Coach of the Year for volleyball.

The Dogs are all registered Labrador Retrievers. Magic is a fourteen year old white lab. Rocky is a fourteen year old chocolate lab that has bred several times. We took the pick of the liters for the first breedings to get Jake and Lucky who are both chocolate labs and half brothers. Jake bred with a different female and we have Shadow who is Jake's son and is also a chocolate lab and our youngest dog. Shadow got to breed and that is where Donald and Katie got Maxwell and Hunter. Our dogs go everywhere with us on the ranch. Lucky, Jake and Shadow go with me on all my horse rides.

The Horses

Buck is a big champagne colored gelding who is the leader of the gelding herd. He is very smart and a good leader. He is Steve's horse and works best for him but anyone can ride Buck as he is patient and seems to know when a little kid is on him.

Benjie is a black gelding and he and Buck were our first two horses. Benjie is Mr. Personality but has the high ring bone which is a joint problem and causes him to limp.

Rudy is almost twenty and he is red chocolate with a flaxen mane and tail and looks like a surfer. I can get on Rudy anytime, anywhere and he will do anything I ask him to do. He is a very special horse and gets special treatment because he is such a hard keeper. I give him extra food but he is always thin. I got him when he was nine and he was very hyper and filled with energy and a big handful. Before we became so close he got scared during an evening ride and did a 180 turn so fast he left me in the dirt and never looked back. I got back on him just to show him who was boss. Ha! One of the people at the place that we were boarding said maybe that was not the horse for me which only made me more determined to ride this beautiful animal with all the spirit. I was once riding Rudy up by the fence after winter and the deer had broken a wire and it was coiled in the grass. Neither Rudy nor I saw the wire until Rudy stepped into the coil and I heard his foot hit the wire. I looked down and tried to back him out and Rudy did exactly what I asked him to do but it soon became apparent that no matter what we did the wire was not coming off. I got off, got his foot out and then found a rock so I could crawl back up. Rudy was perfect during the entire episode which could have been such a catastrophe had he gotten scared. My most recent adventure was riding him into the forest while there was still snow and ice. He slipped and we were horizontal to the ground and I knew we were going to fall. I still have no idea how he did it but he caught himself and slid back under me to put us both "back in the saddle". It all happened so fast, I have no idea how he saved us both. I ride Rudy almost every day. He likes to run and has a very animated gait. He always looks forward to these rides and even helps get the bit in his mouth.

Tie is Mr. Mischievous and once ate a hole right through the middle of a piece of plywood. He is black and looks almost like Benjie. He tries to sneak out the gate when it is open. He is always the first horse to come see me when I walk into the pasture. When I turn the horses out to graze the front lawn he is looking at the trash cans to see if there is something good in there.

Mister is deep chocolate with a flaxen mane and tail and is very fancy although he is not the smartest horse out there. Mister still thinks that having to back up so he will stand still is part of the getting on process. Once I am on him he is a wonderful horse to ride. He is a fast walking go anywhere horse. His gait is really animated and he really moves out. I was once riding him when one of the reins broke, it had a screw and the screw came out. Mister was totally patient and did not seem to care. I rode him for a while with only the one rein and he was fine but I thought if I had a problem that would not be good so I got off and walked him back to fix the rein.

Rock is a rich brown and white spotted mountain horse and has a soft brown eye and is very smart. He used to be the leader of the yearlings until

Aggie got ready to deliver her foal and then I put him with the geldings. Rock pushed Buck for leadership of the herd but Buck is just too smart and too tough. That whole show of who would be the new boss was very interesting to watch because they are both extremely smart and tough. Buck would chase Rock but Rock was just a little younger and a little faster and just went fast enough to keep Buck from catching him. I never saw Buck actually get him but they played that game for two weeks. Buck remains the undisputed leader of all the horses.

Dancer is Tiffany's half brother. He is just turning four and ready to be trained. He is a bit skittish and stand offish but a beautiful deep bay horse.

Blue is black with three white feet and is one of the rescue horses. He is also just turning four. He is just darling and will follow me everywhere and have his nose in everything.

Josie is solid black with perfect exquisite features. She is proud, very striking and has very high leg action and has the thickest mane and tail. She is a bit wild but much better than when we first got her. She is ready to be trained also.

Tiffany is as big as Buck and the leader of the mare herd. She is a dark bay with a black mane and tail. She is very independent but demands her attention anytime we are out there. She likes to be rubbed and get her attention. She has an annoying habit of pawing the ground when she wants something.

Aggie is gray with a black mane, tail and legs. Aggie is the mother of FOG. Aggie is always the first horse to come over to the fence. She stands in the corner and waits for me to come out every day. She loves attention and is truly beautiful. She is pretty aggressive with all the other horses.

Fog, short for Flat Out Gorgeous, is just turning three and right now is all black with one white foot but she gets a little grayer each year like her mom. Fog is still pretty independent and always comes to see if we have carrots but quickly loses interest if we have none.

Regal is our newest mare and she is truly beautiful. She is deep chocolate with a flaxen mane and tail and has the most loving personality. Regal is also the look alike twin of Mister even though they are not related. She is very easy going and so loving. I am just starting to work with her as she is only green broke at this point.

The Other Animals

Puff is the tiger gray cat with white feet and white bib that adopted us. She was annoyed this morning because Buck was eating the grass right outside the tack room and looking in at her.

We have thirteen chickens that are buff orpingtons, gold sex links, Wyandotte, and Rhode Island reds. We have one incredible rooster —Godzilla because he is so much bigger than all the other chickens. The only other chickens with names are: Spice, the black and white Wyandotte, No Butt because she has no tail feathers like the other chickens and Gimp because she has a hurt leg.

Manly was our first bull and bred with Midnight and White Face. Manly is the father of Costco, a heifer, from Midnight. Licorice is a steer from White Face. Costco and Licorice were born in April this year. Road Block is last years' daughter of White Face. We sold Manly in August of last year and bought another younger Black Angus bull that is at Tom and Donna's until they are ready to turn them out. Tom and Donna are feeding and taking care of him for us. Tom named this new bull Steve but we changed his name to BB for Bush Bull. BB came to our place in May of this year. We trailered him over, opened the gate and he walked out to find the girls. He got half way across the pasture and called them. White Face came trotting over like the obedient girl. It is always strange to me that cattle just accept each other. There is no chasing, no dominance issues like with the horses. We now have the herd of six with BB, the two cows, last year's yearling heifer and the two new calves.

Chapter 2

HOW DID WE GET HERE

We bought Buck and Benjie in 2000 and had gotten our trailer and then the F550 so we could trailer horses to parks every weekend. I found that I loved being around the horses. I loved the quiet and the peace of being out in the country. I loved the challenge of trying new places and new adventures.

I was born and raised in Southern California and spent my entire life there. I watched it change from orange groves, avocado groves and strawberry fields into freeways and houses and lots of people. I started thinking about retirement and how I saw that picture. I thought about sitting in my house and waiting for someone to go out to lunch or dinner with and waiting in line for the movies and for the restaurants and sitting in traffic on freeways trying to go five miles away. I was tired of playing tennis and hated golf. All my life I had been active and could not imagine just sitting in the city. After we got the horses it became very apparent that I wanted enough land to live on so we could have our horses. I wanted a place where the cops did not come by and tell me our truck was too big to park on the street and the association said we could only paint our house a certain color and we had to have the design of our yard approved and we could not leave our garage door open. Now, don't get me wrong, these are all good things that help keep the neighborhood and housing costs up but that is not how I saw my retirement.

Steve and I decided we wanted to live in the country and have a garden and park our truck where ever we wanted or leave the wheel barrel out until we finished a project. I wanted the horses right there with me. Steve tried to tell me that it would be a lot of work. I told him I had never been afraid of work but this would be on our time and what we chose to do and when we chose to do it. We knew we could not afford property in Southern California but we wanted to stay on the coast. I had visited Steve's family in Texas. I had been so excited when we got there. Oh boy—they had a riding lawn mower for this huge lawn. That would be fun, so I offered to mow the lawn, trying to be the good fiancé at the time. Ha. The riding lawn mower was broken. I did this entire, huge lawn with a push mower. It was over a hundred degrees, the bugs were bad and when I came in they made me take a bath in bleach because of the chiggers and ticks. You have to be kidding me. I did not want to live down there. So, we started looking in Oregon and Washington for land for our horses. We packed the two dogs and took off to look at several places where we had appointments. We found a place with this doublewide modular home with a barn and fences on seventy eight acres down a dirt road with a mailbox a quarter of a mile away. It said horse ranch. That was for us. Each place we looked at we compared to this place so it finally became very clear that this was the place we wanted. We filled out loan papers and were told we qualified only to be told three weeks later that the underwriters would not carry the mortgage on undeveloped land and this place was on five separate parcels. We fell out twice and we were crushed. We finally found someone to finance it and we were excited.

Since the day we arrived we have been working every day to fix or improve this place. The well went dry and we had to trench and install an underground water storage vault. The water heater fell through the floor and the water damage destroyed the wash room, kitchen and part of the family room. The shower developed an internal water leak and the wall disintegrated and ruined the guest room walls and bathroom floor and we had to replace the shower, the floors, the walls, the carpets and paint everything. The horses went right through rotten fences. There was no water or working electricity to the horse tanks and I had to drag 150 feet of hose up and down the hill in the middle of winter and break two inches of ice so they could drink. With the dirt road out front the dust is unbelievable. I have put most of the knick knacks away because it is just too hard to dust and I do not have time.

In the time we have been here we have had the most snow ever recorded, the 3rd most snow ever recorded, the third least amount of snow ever recorded, the most snow in November, the most snow in December and the most rain ever in April and the most days below twenty degrees ever recorded. We have had days above 114 degrees at our house, days below zero degrees with the wind howling, two feet of snow over night and so much rain we have "seasonal creeks". We had two inches of ice everywhere and it was so bad three of my horses slipped and fell. I fell three times in one day but fortunately never got hurt. Steve got on the computer and ordered both of us strap on cleats. In the winter time I never go out without my cleats. I had a problem with them sliding off so I used the twine from hay bales and tied it around my boots to keep the cleats on. Steve got me better cleats with Velcro to keep them on my boots and I no longer have a problem with slipping. We have had summers with little black annoying bugs that got in our eyes, nose, mouth and ears and I finally had to make nets to go over our faces. We have had hornets that are annoying. We have had grasshoppers so bad that I used blocks of wood to try to squash them in the garden. I killed hundreds and it did not make a difference. We have had great gardens and lousy gardens. I have learned that I do not need so many zucchini plants and only plant the things we love to eat. I have learned that the chickens will eat just about anything.

Now, all of that being said, we love this place. Every day is a challenge. We fix anything that is broken and then we go on with our plan for the day. The view is incredible and the wildlife is sensational. It is peaceful and quiet and we live on a dirt road and mostly only see the cars of the few neighbors that go by. About the time we get tired of winter, it is spring and about the time we get tired of summer, it is fall.

I have learned so many things since we got here that it is like a whole new job and life and I would not trade. We are on a very strict budget and have big discussions about the merits of anything we buy and how essential it is to what we have to do. I keep detailed records of every cent we spend so we do not go over budget.

This is a very tough life out here and definitely not for the weak or lazy. I have a whole new respect for farmers and ranchers. So much of their lives depend on the weather and the crops and none of that can really be planned for. This is a hard life and I love the challenges. My family all says I work too hard but I cannot even imagine just sitting around and I have no desire to travel. I love the horses, dogs and all the animals. I always tell everyone that I had not realized this place came with a built in gym membership. I walk all day and I lift bales of hay, shovel manure and still cook, clean and do the household stuff. Each day has its own challenges. Each day has daily chores and each day has room for projects we want to do.

I have planted gardens and I learned how to can peaches and pears and I learned how to deal with horses with colic and cows having birth problems. I plan, organize, think, use my math skills, use my strength and adapt every day to a new situation. I am no longer afraid to knock out a wall—I know how to fix it. Just about anything that happens has a solution and we have to work it out and make a plan to solve so many different events as our lives change each day. As I get older, I am still losing strength but I learn to overcome and deal with whatever I have to do. I get on and off my horses on a mounting block but I am still riding almost every day. We hire kids to do some of the stuff we can no longer do. If I cannot lift something I break it down to pieces that I can lift or get a better tool to help me do what I need to do. I still love it here. When we had so much snow that my RTV would not go up the hill and I knew the horses still had to be fed I got a snow shovel and tied down flakes of hay and walked through two feet of snow dragging hay up the hill and I had to do that several times to feed them all but they did get fed.

When we got here we had two dogs and three horses. We came from city life with a house cleaner that came in twice a month and a gardener that came every week. We used to go out to eat several times a week and to the movies at least once a week. Now, we have five dogs, thirteen horses, six head of cattle, fourteen chickens and a cat that adopted us. I am the house cleaner and the house is fortunate to get cleaned although I do dishes everyday and we are the only gardeners. In the spring I let the horses out around the house to mow, trim and fertilize the yard. I cook every day because town is forty-five minutes away and we do not take the time to go to the movies. We wait until the movie comes out on DVD and gets to a low price and then buy it. My priorities have changed. Feeding and taking care of the animals is always first, house and projects come after that. When I worked I had nice clothes and wore make up every day. Now, I wear sweats, muck boots, t-shirts and work jackets and gloves. Expensive clothes are no longer important. I always have hay in my hair and on my clothes. My shirts always have horse snot or mud or something on them but I love it here. Garrett came over the other day to share his chipper shredder and wanted to come in for a chat. He looked at me and said "you have poop on your face". I had been out shoveling manure from the horse stalls. He told me I should not sling it so hard. We both laughed.

We have some delightful neighbors that will help us any time we have a problem and we help them when they need us. When we first got here I saw Garrett and Tom out in the field and drove my RTV out to meet them. They were not sure what to think of me but they invited us to their barbecue. We had a wonderful time and thought we were good company. They did not invite us to the next party. I saw Tom again and said "wow, I was only invited to one party and then I was cut off the guest list—was I that bad?" They all laugh at me because I am such a city girl but I am learning. I so love all these special neighbors. What a great group of people.

My family comes to visit. They all help when they come. Kym, my brother, and Jessie his daughter, helped plant the garden and some special trees. Kym used the weed whacker when it was so hot; I thought he would pass out. Kym helped build the horse sun shelters. He saved the turkey and he loves to ride the horses. At night he plays the guitar and sings the songs we grew up to while I do dishes. Lad brings his kids and they ride horses and Lad works in the garden—last year he saved my whole garden by hand weeding around each plant. We had gotten so busy with all the building that we just could not do it all. Lad also plants the planters around the house and puts great flowers in them that I love so much. Ty, my oldest brother and role model, takes delightful walks with us and we play bridge at night—I am not a good bridge player but they do not mind and his wife Kris is the best at finding things that need to be done. She also saved my garden one year. She is delightful. Kit, my sister, helps me keep my sanity. She is the most generous, kind person I know. We talk on the phone a lot and she always sends me fun gifts. How did I get so fortunate to have such a wonderful family?

Chapter 3

THE MOVE

We had sold the house in Southern California in April but rented back until school was out—about June 19th and we had to be out of the house by the 21st. What a roller coaster ride but that is another story.

I had put everything I wanted to hand carry in the bath tub upstairs and told the movers to leave it. I had been packing for months yet it took five movers and two days to pack up the rest of our household belongings. The movers had been there on June 17th and 18th. On the 21st of June, 2004, our move out day, we put dog beds on the platform in the rear seat of our F550. We loaded the back of the truck with all the stuff I thought we would need until our "stuff" from the movers arrived. I had packed foam pads to sleep on, sheets, pillows, two plates, two sets of utensils, one cooking pot, my black cast iron skillet, my personal stuff of clothes, make up, important papers and Steve's personal stuff. I had wanted to take some of our hanging plants but they would not fit. I dug up some of the cymbidium orchids and threw them into a plastic bag. Rocky and Magic jumped into the back seat with their beds—they always travel so well. The new owners showed up and we gave them all the keys—wow, that felt final. We drove out to the military base where we boarded our three horses. We hooked up the trailer, loaded several bales of hay into the front compartment of the horse trailer, cleaned out our tack locker and loaded the horses—Buck, Benjie and Rudy. These horses are Rocky Mountain

Registered horses. They are bred for a smooth, comfortable gait and their temperament which is second to none. They are easy going and not much bothers them. We were off on our new adventure. It was sad to leave the state I had grown up in but very exciting to be on this great adventure.

Hauling a trailer was still fairly new to us and as we got to the grape vine on the freeway we were delighted to have all that power to pull up that hill while we were hauling three horses and a big part of our life in luggage but we noticed a flashing red light in the rear view mirror. Not good. We pulled over and sure enough, he was after us. We could not understand why because we were not speeding and we had checked all the lights and did not understand what we had done wrong. The officer came to my side of the truck since the freeway was moving pretty fast. He asked me if we knew why we were pulled over and I just said "because you wanted to see the horses, they are Rocky Mountain Horses and they are awesome." He said no and then I said "oh then you probably wanted to look at the F550. There are very few of them that are used just like a truck and it is an incredible piece of machinery." He looked at me like I was nuts—maybe I am. It turns out that you cannot be in that lane while pulling a trailer. We were not in the fast lane or even the 2nd of 5 lanes but we were over one lane too far. We obviously did not know that—we have a lot to learn. It must have been our lucky day because he let us go with a warning—maybe he thought no one could be that oblivious. I was very grateful.

The dogs travel well, jumping out every time we stop to get a drink and do their business. They are incredible dogs, just happy to be with us and on a road trip. The horses also travel really well and were the hit at every stop we made. We drop down the bars in the windows and they stick their heads out for carrots and sips of water and watch the world. In fact, at one rest stop we felt the horses had been standing for so long that we needed to get them out. There is an area that says pet area and all animals must be on a leash. I guess that is us. We had our horses on leashes—halters and lead ropes. We walked them around and they were happy to be out. People looked at us as if we had lost it but they all wanted to pet the horses.

We made our goal for the first night, a spot in northern California, and made arrangements to keep our horses at a great horse hotel. The lady was delightful, ready for us and we felt good leaving them there. We stayed in a hotel that allowed dogs. We brought in their beds and their folding cage and they just slept right there. They tell us when they need to go out. We were exhausted and happy to have a shower and a bed to sleep in for the night. The next day we got up, retrieved our horses and set out for our second day of driving. We were planning on stopping at our friends place in Seattle but we got a call from the moving company and they said our "stuff" would be there tomorrow. Oh my, so much for the leisurely trip. We got out the map and changed our course and headed for our destination in Washington. Steve kept driving and we were both exhausted. After 16 hours my head kept bobbing like one of those bobble head dolls and no matter how hard I tried, I could not keep my eyes open. We got to the major town and still had to drive through there and then out into the country to get to our place. We had only been there twice when we were buying the place. It was now one in the morning and I was the bobble head and Steve had been driving forever. It was dark and there are no lights out in the country on the dirt roads. It was darker than dark. Steve did find our house and we pulled up at two in the morning. We got out, the dogs got out and we went to look at the horse stalls. They were dirty. We cleaned them out and closed the doors so they would be limited to the twelve by twelve stalls since we could not see anything outside. We had brought buckets and we filled them with water and hung them on the wall. We put food in the stalls and put the horses in their stalls with water and food. We moved our survival stuff into the house and just put our pads on the floor in the living room so we could hear the horses if there was a problem. I think we passed out around 3:30 in the morning. How on earth were we supposed to know that the sun comes up at 4:45 in the morning in June? Sure enough, it came blasting through the window to wake us up after a little over an hour of sleep. It was ok because I was so excited I could not stand it. We got up and walked out to see the horses. The previous owner had rented back and moved out in May so nothing had happened since May. We opened the back barn door and the grass was up to our waist—oh my. We opened the stalls to the run outs and they were not bad. There was a huge fenced in area that we call the 1 by 2 which is 100 by 200 feet. That had a lot of grass on it. We left the horses in the run outs because they had never been turned loose to graze all day. We did let them out for a while but had to monitor that. Our "stuff" from the movers was supposed to get there the next day. We spent the day trying to get organized and ready for movers. We did have a refrigerator because it was left with the house. I had brought food for a couple days so we unpacked what we had and went to town to get more food supplies. The horses and dogs did well while we were gone. The next day we called the movers but they said it would not be there until the next week. Ok, we can get the carpets cleaned and ride horses and check the place out. We can deal with that. It turns out, the movers did not come for three weeks—they could not find our stuff. The movers had parked the trailer in the back of their lot and just left it there. It had taken a whole big trailer from front to back with all our stuff. We had given things to friends, taken stuff to good will, threw many loads of stuff out, had a garage sale and still had a whole trailer of stuff. If you haven't noticed, we seem to be pack rats—we keep everything and think we will use it. In all actuality, we really do use most of the stuff sooner or later. At any rate, the movers had parked the trailer and forgotten where it was. They could not find it. They gave some lame excuse after another. I was really pleased we had packed our little survival stuff and we were ok—except for the horses but that is another story.

Chapter 4

OUR FIRST THREE WEEKS WITHOUT OUR STUFF

After getting up that first day without our "Stuff"—stuff being all our household belongings and all of Steve's tools and yard equipment—basically everything we owned except the little survival things that I had brought with us for our first couple days, we saddled up horses and ponied Benjie. I had been smart enough to put all horse tack, food, buckets and equipment in the trailer. We had gotten Red Chocolate Rudy, a registered Kentucky Mountain Horse, when we realized that Benjie would keep falling and we did not think he was safe to ride but he was part of the family and Mr. Personality and just gorgeous. We took the horses and the two dogs for a ride around the seventy-eight acres. We checked fences and gates and tried to determine if we could safely let horses out. The fences were old and the deer had loosened wires during the winter. The place was beautiful and there was grass everywhere. We would have to monitor our horses since they had never been out to free graze since we got them. We let them into the 100 by 200 corral for about an hour and they started taking down that waist high grass. We would put them back into the stalls with run outs and then back out to graze. The previous owner had left us a big one hundred gallon water tank but we did not have hoses yet so we used the buckets that we brought with us to fill it up. We hung the buckets with water in the stalls. We started to make a list of the things we would need just to survive. The most important thing was to keep the horses contained and safe. We could adjust to anything for us but we had to constantly be aware of what was going on with the horses. One of the first things we would need is a source of hay. We had brought several bales with us but needed to figure out how to get more. We found one of the farm stores and bought about ten bales to keep us going while we figured it out. We were not feeding as much as normal because they were grazing but we could not let them graze all the time until they got used to it and the fences we had seen were not safe to keep them contained. We could not fix the fences because all Steve's tools were in our moving van that was not here and the moving company could not find our moving truck.

We had bought our horses through a trainer in Seattle, who became a good friend of ours. We had told him that we were moving to this ranch and ultimately wanted ten horses so that when family came to visit we would have horses for everyone. Well, we had been talking to him and he had bought four yearlings. Aggie who is now gray with black mane, tail and legs and Rock who is a gorgeous brown and white paint with soft brown eyes and Tiffany who is a big bay and then Music Man who we were going to board for a woman who had bought him. We had also agreed to buy Mister from their friends. Mister is a deep chocolate with flaxen mane and tail. Our trainer had kept these horses for a month and was waiting for us to get here so he could get rid of them. About the third day we were here he called and said he was bringing all of them including Neron and Sandy. Neron and Sandy belonged to him and we were just going to let them graze and grow up a bit on our place. Our trainers have a very well set up place on five acres with an arena and round pens and stalls. It is very nice place but seven horses is a lot of horses to board for someone and he was ready to give them to us. We told him we had nothing at our place but thought we had spots for the horses. I got the feeling he was bringing them no matter what. So, on about our fourth day at our new ranch we got seven more horses to add to our three. What on earth was I thinking? Our friend helped us put them in the places we thought they could stay. He visited for a while and left. We learned lesson number one, do not stand in a group of horses and hand out carrots. Buck bit Music Man on the nose and made a nasty cut that was bleeding all over. We got it stopped, called the trainer who was about forty-five minutes out and he said "it will probably heal on its own, if not see the vet." It was apparent we were on our own with ten horses, fences that were only so so, no tools, no bed, and just not much of anything. We obviously had to adjust. The previous owner had an area he called the sacrifice area because he put the horses in there and they ate all the grass so he was sacrificing the grass in that area. First thing we realized was that we did not have enough water tanks and would shortly run out of food. We went to our local farm store and got four more water tanks and hoses to get water to the tanks. We had all the geldings in the sacrifice area and we had the four yearlings in the stalls with run outs.

The second or third day we realized that the cut on Music Man was not doing well so we loaded him up and took him to the vet. They cleaned it out and it had dead skin and hair in it so the cut became bigger. The vet cleaned it all out and pulled out dead tissue and Music Man got stitches and antibiotic that we had to give to him several times every day. This is a yearling that is not broke and barely handled up to this point. The good news about that was that we worked with him every day and he got much better. A couple days later Rock got kicked and opened up his leg. We went back to the vet, stitches and antibiotic. The vets now knew us by our first names. Both these horses had to go back to get stitches out.

The second or third day at our new ranch I noticed that Neron was on the wrong side of the fence and he had cut his legs on the wire. He obviously rolled too close to the fence and somehow went under it. The good news was that the cuts were not too bad and he had stayed right there with all the other horses. Sometime in the first week or so someone nailed Sandy and he had a six inch cut down his chest. It did not look deep and did not seem to get infected. No vets for those incidents.

Rock had been castrated shortly before he got to us. It had healed but he still thought he was the all enforcing stallion and leader of the herd. He was chasing the girls around and Tiffany had taken down a board on the fence and gone through it and we were afraid they would go through the fences or get hurt so we put the girls in one of the run outs and left Rock in the one by two to get some exercise. He is beautiful and I stood on the porch and watched him. He stood close to the end fence and called to the girls. They answered him. Rock ran down to the other end and ran back as fast as he could and called again—oh good he stopped. He ran back to the other end and came racing back again—he stopped again. The third time it became very apparent that he was not going to stop—not good. He hit that end fence, never even jumped, just hit it solid and the rotten six by six and all the boards collapsed and Rock never stopped. He got up by the girls and pranced around and was so proud of himself. Holy cow. We captured him and put him back with the girls in the run outs for the stalls. We went to look at the damage. It was very apparent that several of the six by sixes were rotten and so were several of the boards. We stood there with no tools, no stuff, nothing and tried to decide what to do. Do we buy twelve foot steel panels, do we tear down the whole fence, do we try to fix it and what is the least expensive and best thing to do. We walked around and pushed the six by six posts and tested the boards. We needed at least eight to ten posts, a couple rail road ties, and several two by eight boards and since most of it was rotten we would have to put electric wire on it—we had no choice. I called the moving company and told them we had horses going through fences and we had no tools because they were all in our stuff which they could not find. They finally agreed to give us $300 to get some tools. You have got to be kidding but it would be better than nothing. We went back to town and got two inch electric tape, things to hang it on and a battery operated drill, post hole diggers, screws, the wood we needed and came back and started fixing. We cannot keep yearlings locked up in stalls with run outs. They need room to exercise.

This place came with a working hot walker. Of course, none of our horses had ever been on a hot walker but we had to get some exercise somehow and if they could run through the wooden fence what would happen to the wire fence that was sagging—we could not turn them loose on that fenced sixty acres. How would we ever get them back? We put the yearlings on the hot walker. Tiffany, Aggie and Music Man did very well. Rock, who is very smart and now knows he can go through fences and thinks he is super horse took about three trips around the hot walker. Three seems to be his evaluation number. On the third trip, he bolted straight up the road beside the hot walker. Holy cow—now what? He hit the end of that rope and thankfully the previous owner had replaced all the rope with new rope. He hit the end of that rope at full force, being the super horse he was, it pulled him backwards and he basically flipped on his back and the rope held. He was on his knees and the walker was almost dragging him but definitely pulling on his head. He got up, shook his head and started walking with everyone else—ok, so he was not super horse. It took him down a peg or two and he learned. The best news was that he was not hurt, he had not broken the machine, and he had just learned a valuable lesson. He was still the herd leader, he was still very smart and he was still full of himself but he was learning. It took us several days to replace posts, boards and secure that one by two and hook up the electric tape. We put the yearlings out there and they hit that electric tape and squealed and everyone ran. I think that group hit that tape about three times and then never touched the fence again which was a good thing because I still think the whole thing is rotten and even I could probably walk through it.

We had separated Neron and Sandy from the rest of the geldings because they had both gotten hurt and they were not our horses. We had them in stalls with the run outs. We let them out to run around the one by two. Neron was a huge handful. He was four. He was big, strong, really beautiful, and had this incredible gait but he was a flake and hard to deal with. Sandy was a palomino color with white mane and tail and he was really striking. He was also a handful and dumber than dumb. We changed his name to DD because he was dumber than dumb. That horse hit the electric tape at least six times a day. He never got it. We had trouble catching him so I ran him, he never stopped running. I could sit down and he kept running. He was beautiful and fun to watch but what do we do with him? We gave them back at the end of the summer. I told the trainer that I had to go back to work for a year and Steve would be here by himself so our friend came and got Neron and Sandy. He ended up sending Sandy back to the original owner because no one could do anything with him. Neron they sold to another friend and they showed him and he did really well. It was nice to be down to eight horses. All but Music Man were ours so if they got hurt or out or whatever, it was all on us.

We still did not have our stuff or our tools except for the few things we bought to try to fix fences and try to keep the horses contained. We were still sleeping on foam pads on the floor and every morning we would wake up and giggle and say "I wonder what the horses did last night." We had the yearlings in a thirty-six by forty eight foot corral with one stall and we would let them out into the one by two or put them on the hot walker. They were darling but basically wild. Both Rock and Music Man got better because when they were cut and on antibiotics we had to disinfect or wrap or give medicine to them every day so they got more used to being handled and more secure with us. One morning when I went out to feed they had knocked out one of the boards but they were still there. One evening, just after dark, when Steve and I got home from getting hay and the yearlings were still in the one by two we could not see them but we could hear this strange sound. It went whoosh, quiet, whoosh. What the heck. We walked out to see what was going on and all four of the yearlings came over to see us. We had bought this egg butt horse ball toy that they loved to play with. Music Man and Rock played tug of war with it and carried it and ran with it. It had a big handle and Rock had stepped in between the handle and the ball and this ball was attached to his leg. None of them were panicked or scared but it was not right. They all walked up together, mentally supporting Rock and stopped in front of us. We picked up Rock's foot and took the ball off and you could almost hear them say "see, I told you they would fix it." They were happy to have the problem solved and ready for dinner. What a crack up. There are so many breeds of horses that would have just gone ballistic and maybe even gotten hurt but these Rocky Mountain Horses are so calm and easy going. It really is amazing.

One morning I got up and looked up the hill and saw all these horses running around up the hill. I was angry, whose horses were on our property—oh dear, those are our horses, how did they get out. My neighbor called and told me my horses were up by her house and they were not being very respectful. I woke Steve up and we got halters and whips and tried to decide how to catch horses that were free in a sixty acre pasture with lousy fences. I still have no idea how they got out. They had somehow undone the gate latch and they were so excited to be out and they were running around and bucking and kicking and having a wonderful time. We walked up the hill and Steve got a halter on Buck and I got a halter on Benjie and we started walking them down the hill. They all followed the herd leader and were actually pretty good about the whole thing.

One day I looked out into the pasture and said: "that is the ugliest horse I have ever seen." I knew it was not one of ours but it was running across our pasture. It had this gangly, awkward run and this huge, ugly head. It got to our fence, stopped and standing flat footed jumped and cleared the fence. Oh my gosh, that is a moose. It just continued on its way across the field, totally oblivious to everything. Nothing was going to mess with that animal. It was huge and seemed to realize it owned the world.

We bought twelve of the six rail, twelve foot steel panels and made a circle in the sixty acre pasture. It took us two hours to set it up. We took the yearlings out there one by one to let them graze. They were a handful to lead and we were very inexperienced. We left them out there for an hour and they demolished that whole area. The next day we moved the circle and they demolished that. It did not take us long to realize that if it took us two hours to move it and took them one hour to demolish the grass, it was not a productive idea. We wanted to get horses out to graze but the fences were not good.

It was about that time that the well went dry because we left the water filling the horse tank and it ran over. We called the previous owner and he said "I wondered when you would do that." What the heck does that mean? It turns out that our hand dug well could not possibly have passed the four hour draw down but the real estate agents said it had passed and it was fine. The previous owner came over to show Steve how to turn off the pump and how to reset after a couple hours so the well could rejuvenate. We did not care because we loved this place but it did present a problem. We do have to be careful with water. That was the beginning of our thought process on how to fix the water problem. The very next summer was the one that we spent the whole summer putting in the water vault at the top of the hill but that is another story.

We had learned that we must be careful with the water. We could turn on the hose but we must never walk away in case we forgot it. We could only do two loads of clothes per day; we could not water the lawn because it used too much water. We were ok but we just had to be aware and be careful. The previous owner said that out biggest chance of running out of water would be December to February when the ground froze hard and the underground water did not quickly fill the well.

The previous owner used to raise Arabian horses and at one time had 35 of them. There was no shelter or shade of any kind out there. We asked him how his horses did out there and he said they never had a problem. In the middle of that first summer it got to be 110 degrees and it was blistering. The horses were dragging. We had to have shade. So, everything else stopped and we designed a frame that would hold up a twelve by twenty tarp and bought the wood and the tarp. We started building. The horses thought we were out there for them and they were constantly in the middle of what we were trying to do. They are very social and curious. It took us three days in that blistering heat but we put up the tarp and laced it all around. The horses loved it and would stand under it all the time when they were not eating. They slept under it and everyone had his spot as the pecking order went. Buck stood where he wanted to stand and everyone else found a spot around him. The yearlings had the one stall and I fixed an area in the barn for Neron and Sandy. The yearlings were always together. They slept outside in a circle. When it was feeding time they stood inside with their noses sticking through the bars. They were incredibly cute.

We went through some major money that first summer. We were just trying to survive and keep the horses safe. We had to adjust for collapsing fences, the incredible heat, the lack of water and how to get food for winter that is cheaper than by the bale and trips to the vet to fix injured horses. Our vet told us who had the best alfalfa in the valley and we got thirty-six ton delivered and stacked. I felt better knowing we would have hay through the winter. We learned a lot that first summer but it was a constant adjustment and survival time. At the end of the summer we realized that we needed more money and I had to go back to work for one more year. Steve would stay here with the animals and just survive. We increased the minutes on the cell phone to 2000 minutes and we talked every day.

Before I went back to work we decided that we would build the building we had dreamed we would have. Steve needed a shop and I needed my exercise room so we designed the building of our dreams and found we could not afford it. We started taking things off until we got to a price we could afford. We contracted with a company to build it while I was still working so Steve could help and have something to do besides take care of the horses. Good thing we put the building up when we did because now, there is no way we could financially do it. We had the building built and to save money we decided to finish the interior ourselves as we get free time. Seven years later and we are still working on the interior—not much free time out here. In the country there is always something you did not anticipate each day. So, we get up, see what needs to be fixed and then do what the plan for the day really was.

I got my horse ride in every day. I could ride right out the front gate and go for hours. Now this was indeed the dream that I had always wanted. It was quiet, peaceful, and incredibly beautiful and almost no traffic on the dirt road that was out in front of our place. There is plenty of wild life and always something new happening each day.

Chapter 5

BUCK, BENJIE AND RUDY

*I*t all started in the year 2000. All my life I had wanted a horse and to live in the country. I had a particularly bad coaching year and my husband said: "It's time to start looking for your horse." I was dumbfounded and told him I was too busy with my teaching and coaching but he was insistent. He said: "If you keep waiting until you are not busy you will never get a horse and be young and physically able to enjoy it if you do get one." Steve started looking on the internet to find a horse. He finally showed me a picture of this big, beautiful buckskin horse with a white blaze and a dark mane and tail. Steve, my husband, said this was a Rocky Mountain Horse. What the heck is that? I had never heard of the breed. He went on to explain that these were gaited horses meaning that they had this smooth movement faster than a walk and you did not bounce around. He also said they were bred for their temperament and easy disposition meaning that they were calm horses. Well, that sounded good. I was getting close to retirement and did not have time to be falling off horses at my age. He told me they were in Washington, two states away. I said: "seriously, there have to be good horses that are close to us. Why do we have to go so far away to find a horse?" He said he liked this horse and was intrigued by the breed and he was going to see it, whether or not I went. Well, there was the challenge, I had to go plus I did not want to be left behind.

I had told these people that we were looking for good trail horses to ride and that I was getting too old to be falling off horses. I wanted to ride

Buck and they had another black gelding named Benjie. When we got there we looked at the horses and they were beautiful. Both Buck and Benjie were four year old registered Rocky Mountain Horses and Benjie was also registered Kentucky Mountain. I got on Buck and the trainer got on Benjie. They lived on five acres in a neighborhood full of houses so we had to ride a ways to get to a trail. We started off on our walk. Everything was going fine until three kids came flying around a corner on trail bikes. Oh boy, I thought I was a goner because both of these horses would surely explode. Neither horse did anything. They just stood there and watched. Well, that is not too bad. We continued our ride through the streets with cars, people, bikes and other distractions. We finally got to the forest and twenty feet away this four wheel off road vehicle came flying through the air. Again, I thought that would be it but again, these horses just stood quietly and watched. Incredible and I just said sold—these were the horses for us. I told Steve that if we got one we had to get both because if I had a horse he would never see me unless he had his own horse so we bought both Buck and Benjie.

That was how it all started. We had them shipped down to us and we boarded them close to our home in southern California and I started riding every day. I think I spent a month of just walking, riding and spending time with Benjie and Steve rode Buck. It took about a month and we got a horse trailer which gave us a lot more options of where we could ride. We had about five parks within an hour of where we boarded and we started trailering every weekend. We soon realized the F250 was not set up to pull a trailer so we got an F550. Holy cow, we could gain speed pulling a trailer up the grapevine, a very long and steep hill on the freeway. Now that was an impressive machine.

We rode down this ravine that got really narrow and Benjie actually crawled out one side while I was riding him. He had this incredibly smooth gait. My friends called him the Cadillac of horses.

Steve asked Buck to go into this strange area that I did not think was safe. Buck took four steps in and the mud sucked up to his knees. I stood there watching and there was no way Steve could safely get off and it was too far to go through so the only way out was to turn around and Buck just stood there and waited to see what was asked of him. Steve slowly turned

Buck to go back. Buck picked up one foot and you could hear the sucking sound of the mud as Buck muscled out of this. He just kept picking up his feet and the muck kept sucking at his legs. Buck never panicked, never did anything but slowly pulled his legs out and walked out of this mess.

The more time we spent with these horses the more we fell in love with them. They were indeed exceptional animals. They were calm, loaded well, trailered well; they were great with the farrier and were happy to be out riding. They were incredible animals. Nothing bothered them. We rode them on trails with cliffs on one side and straight up hills on the other side. We went through water, down canyons, over rocks, through underpasses that were only high enough for us to fit through with cars whizzing by overhead, across narrow wooden bridges and along side roads. Once in a while they would get a little nervous but nothing really upset them.

I was once riding Buck and was turned around to look at his poop and he side stepped and I fell off. I landed right between his front feet and looking up at his nose. He stood there and looked down at me like why was I down there. I had to find a little hill so I could get back on and I forgot to check the cinch. As I started climbing back on the saddle slipped so it was on sideways but I was determined to stay on. I struggled to get up top and got my foot in the other stirrup and pushed down. The whole saddle just rolled back from his side up to the top and he did not care.

Buck is big, bold and beautiful. He is very smart and the leader of our herd. My eight year old niece can ride him and he is gentle. He is 15. 3 hands high and has this tiny little gait that is so smooth to ride and you look at him and cannot believe that huge animal can move like that. He is delightful to watch. He loves Steve because Steve does not take any baloney from him and they look good together.

Benjie had developed a high ring bone and kept falling. He never hurt me and always protected me. He would fall and then get straight back up. He never fell when it was really dangerous but I was worried about him. We tried all kinds of tests to find out his problem but they finally said he had a high ring bone and would limp for the rest of his life. My niece loves him and rides him all the time while she is here but I am much bigger and feel awful riding him because he limps even though the vet has said I cannot hurt him. He has this wonderful heart and I call him Mr. Personality and as long as he does not seem to be in pain he will live with us.

One of my friends calls them the potato chip horse because you cannot have just one. These horses are kind, gentle and just amazing animals. They do not buck, rear or do bad things. There is very little that bothers them. They like attention and they like to go for rides even though they may get a bit barn sour once in a while.

That was the beginning. It did not take long before I realized that I was ready to retire and move to the country so we could have these wonderful animals with us. In 2003 we started looking for a place and in the summer of 2004 we moved to our 78 acres in the country.

When I realized that Benjie would always have a problem we got Rudy. He had a lot more energy and was a lot harder to control than either Benjie or Buck but he was beautiful, walked really fast and I loved him.

Chapter 6

THE DOGS

We had gotten our dogs in southern California and had them down there for about seven years before we moved to our ranch. We have a big, gorgeous, sweet tempered chocolate Labrador retriever named Rocky and a Pure White lab named Magic. They are incredible, loving, beautiful dogs. We had done all the yuppie stuff and taken them to obedience class and agility courses and they got their certificates and little trophies. Magic was so good he was always the good example that the teachers demonstrated with. Both Magic and Rocky love people. Their favorite time was Halloween. Every time the door bell rang, they would run to the door to greet the little kids. Of course they stood eye level with some of them but the kids all loved the dogs. We neutered Magic because he showed some signs of aggressive behavior and we did not want to pass that on in breeding. While traveling up here we had two dog beds in the back seat of the truck. Both dogs jumped in and lay down on their bed and they rode quietly, just happy to be with us on this great adventure.

At the end of our fist summer here we asked the vets if there were any female chocolate labs to breed with and they found us another couple that had a female chocolate lab. They came over to meet our Rocky and loved him and said they would be back when she was ready. The people came with a chocolate lab and we checked her papers to be sure she was not related to Rocky. Rocky got to breed and we said we wanted the pick of the liter. Well, when they were done breeding, they brought their other girl and Rocky bred with her also. There was one liter of ten and one liter of eight. Since our contract was for pick of the liter we got two puppies and they were half brothers and we named them Jake and Lucky. Steve got these puppies in January of that first winter at the ranch by himself while I was down south working. It definitely kept him busy. Fortunately, that first winter was not bad.

We had spent hours training our first two labs and they were so good. We read books and followed the rules and these dogs were the good examples in all the classes. Everyone loved them and admired them. Well, with the new puppies we were so busy all the time, they did not get all that instruction and they just went out the door with us. They ran free on the property but were only out when we were out. We did not realize how unsocialized they were until we tried to put a leash on them. Our old dogs were so excited to be going somewhere but the puppies thought they were being punished. The puppies did not know how to act when people came to see them. Oh dear. We had not done the socialization. They were good, but not like the first two that were perfect.

A couple years passed and a lady saw Rocky in a pet store and asked if we bred with him. We said yes and so Rocky got to breed again but she also had another female and Jake, who was now three years old, got to breed with her other female, who was a famous dock jumper and Jake was a great athlete himself. The puppies from those liters were incredible. Again we asked for pick of the liter because I wanted to give one to my brother and one to my niece. The niece took her dog but my brother felt he could not keep a dog where he lived so we kept the other puppy and named him Shadow. Wow, Shadow is big, bold, hunts, points, brings me deer sheds, catches gophers and moles and brings me any dead animal he finds. He is a great hunter and a beautiful dog.

We had people say they wanted to breed with Shadow who was now three years old so they did and she had ten chocolate puppies. One of my old students Donald and his beautiful, sweet new wife wanted two so we said we would keep them until they could come and get them. So, at our house we had the original two labs that are about fourteen, the two half brothers that are six, the one youngest that is three and then the two puppies. We had the great grandfather, the grandfather, the father and the puppies. I think I am a lot older since the last time we had puppies. Holy cow, what was I thinking? We had these two new puppies, Maxwell and Hunter, for almost a month. They were incredibly cute, fun, and lots of work. We had an indoor day area, an outdoor poop and pee area, a kennel and the other five big dogs with dog beds everywhere. My husband and I tag teamed these darling little guys. They were out in the snow, the rain, the sun and they played, pooped and grew every time they took a nap. We had little harnesses for them and they went for walks and we took them into our enclosed orchard and they ran and tackled and played and chewed everything. They are truly beautiful animals. Donald and Katie were here for five days and they have never had puppies in their lives. They read the books before they got here and did lots of preparation but I do not think anything prepares you for two chocolate lab puppies. They had to rent a car to take them home because they were too big to fit under the seat in an airplane. We helped them set up the car for the long drive with puppies and they said that Maxwell and Hunter traveled very well and were so good and really got into the routine. Amazing. Steve and I slept for a week after they left but I miss the puppies and Donald and Katie. Absolutely delightful people and I am sure they will have lots of fun with these puppies. I talked to Donald and they are doing the yuppie thing just like we did. I am sure Maxwell and Hunter will be much better trained than our dogs but since they live in the city that is important. Katie says they have already annihilated a whole planter of plants. Ah, puppies. You gotta love it.

At any rate, we have five big labs that live in our house. That was never the original plan but I would really be lonely without them. They are with me almost all the time. Jake, Lucky and Shadow go on the horse rides, and they all love to go for our walks in the forest. When we stack or move hay they are all right in the middle of everything looking for mice and jumping up and down and climbing on the layers of the stacked bales of hay. They like to ride on the platform with the hay. They are just a real joy to have around. Shadow brings me all kinds of things like dead animals and old bones. I have tried to throw those things away. Ha! Have you ever tried to throw something away from a lab—they just bring it back. I bury some of their treasures when I think they are not looking. That does not work either—they smell too well and they find it and dig it up. About the only thing that works is to let them carry it home and put it into the trash can. They are pretty persistent and will retrieve anything until they are exhausted. Shadow is always digging for something. We have electronic collars for Jake, Lucky and Shadow so that I can get their attention while we are on horse rides. The dogs are actually pretty good and I do not have to zap them very often.

Chapter 7

THE TRACTOR AND THE RTV

When we finally bought this place we were so excited. We were still working at our jobs in southern California and we were dreaming and planning. We closed on this place in December of 2003 but were committed to our jobs until spring of 2004. I had never lived anywhere but the city. I was clueless. Steve had lived on fifteen acres in Texas and worked with chickens, horses, and a pig and worked around their small farm. The best I could say was that we had pigeons in our back yard, the baby chicks that we always won at the fair and always died and a duck named Quackerdy. My idea with the duck was that ducks are supposed to have water to swim and play in. We knew Quackerdy ate snails—now that was something. He truly annihilated every snail in the back yard. Well, I thought Quackerdy needed water so my brothers and I buried a huge fifty gallon trash barrel in the ground and filled it with water. The top was about even with the ground but he had to be able to get in and out easily so it needed to be filled all the way to the top. Well Quackerdy absolutely loved his "pond". He would hop in, swim in small circles and get out. Of course, he did poop in there and after a while the water got a little disgusting but how do you change it?—small problem. I am not sure how long we had Quackerdy but I do remember that my mom made us take him to the park that had great ponds and lots of ducks. He hoped right in there and seemed to be happy. Of course, you have to realize that this was in the 50's and you could do stuff like that.

Anyway, as Steve and I planned and thought about our "dream place" it became apparent that we would have to have some farm equipment. Steve started doing the research on tractors—we cannot have a farm without a tractor. I started thinking about the seventy-eight acres and how, at my age, was I going to get around this place. I mean, I had to carry horse food and clean up manure and do big jobs like that. Steve is the computer literate, reader, analyzer, study guy that reads everything. He is the kind of guy that will take a computer manual and read it and understand it—holy cow, was I fortunate to have married someone that understands stuff like that. I mean, I am a great idea person—like the duck in the water—but Steve is the guy that does the research and decides how to make it happen. He does the research and decides which of the tractors out there is the best for us. This company also has a little run around four wheel drive utility vehicle that I might like. Oh, yeah, I am loving that. So, we build into our budget that we must have a tractor and this four wheel drive utility vehicle. Those will be two of the first things we get so we can function.

As soon as we got here with our two dogs and three horses we tried to make this place as safe as possible for the horses but we still did not have our household belongings. We really could not do anything else so we found the local tractor dealer and drove down there. I looked at the sales lot with all the tractors and saw one that looked huge to me and jumped up on it to see how it fit and if it looked like I could work it. The sales man, Jack, came out and we started talking. I just liked that tractor but Steve wanted to talk horse power, implements, lifting capacity and other important stuff like that. Jack was great, and not just a salesman, he was part of the community. Later when I had to have my surgery his company sent me flowers at the hospital—I mean wow, talk about being concerned about the people you deal with. I was impressed. Anyway, Jack stood on the tractor step and asked me if I wanted to turn that thing on—are you kidding, we are in the middle of a lot with tractors everywhere and you want me to move this thing? That is not happening but I appreciated the fact he had asked. I looked at the information brochures while Steve and Jack talked about important stuff like power, lifting capabilities and implements. We did get a forty three horsepower tractor with a front loader, box scraper and post hole auger to dig all the holes we would need for fixing all the fences. Wowie zowie they had a three year, no interest payment plan—sign me up for that! Ok, so we got the tractor specifics settled but I needed my four wheel drive vehicle. Jack took us back out to the lot and showed me this incredibly bright orange, little car like vehicle with big wheels to go through the fields. It had a hydraulic lift for the truck bed. You mean, I could fill it with horse manure, drive to the compost pile and then hit this lever and dump it all? I am loving that. It had a cab to keep the snow or rain off of me. It had a windshield with this strange wiper blade. That wiper blade is the only thing I do not understand. It pushes the water up to horizontal and then comes back, well, the water just rolls down where you just cleaned it from. Who could make such an incredible machine and do that? Oh well, if that was the only thing wrong with it, I was all for it. They did not have the super three year plan for that but we had built this into our budget so I was not leaving without it. They said that they would deliver both of them plus the equipment we wanted with it. Oh yeah! I told Jack we wanted all those cool tools at the same time and could he please spend some time with us to explain their operation, in an area with more space to demonstrate how to work this stuff. Of course, Steve rolled his eyes because he could do anything but I felt I wanted the real professional to show me—I work better that way.

Holy cow, let me tell you about these machines. They are truly the best things we ever bought for this place. Since we got here we have bought other attachments for that tractor. We do not use the box scraper much but we use the post hole auger all the time. We got a disk harrow that plows the ground and a rotary rough cutter that cuts the grass or weeds or brush and one of the most important implements of all is the pallet forks. That tractor can lift almost anything. We have a platform that slides onto the pallet forks that was made by the construction crew that built our arena. We use that platform constantly. We load it up with hay and move it. Steve gets on the platform and I lift him up to the highest it will reach, 10 feet, and he puts all the lighting into the arena. We use it to lift one or the other of us up so we can drag snow off buildings. We use it to pick apples from the top of the tree and to help us construct all the animal shelters we have built. We use it to put tarps on top of frames for shade for the horses. We lift long roofing panels up to the roofs of the sheds we are building and we load huge trees to bring up for fire wood. We use it to carry tools and just on and on.

I do find it fascinating that I am the only one that Steve trusts to lift him up to that high level on the platform. Me, the non-mechanical genius and he puts his life in my hands. He is so casual up there and I always tell him to hold on while I am moving it up or down because it does not seem to matter how many times I drive that tractor I always seem to forget which way to push the control lever that controls the tilting up or down or raising or lowering that platform. I have to go through this new learning process every time I drive the tractor. Mostly, I am pretty good but Steve yells if I have him tipped too far. I try hard but basically I truly am not mechanical. I can however see that he is sliding off so I always go very slowly and I think that annoys him but I feel it is so much better than quickly sliding him right off.

We later bought a backhoe that hooks to the back of the tractor. Wow, that is truly impressive. We spent that one whole summer digging a trench with the backhoe and laying pipe and digging the hole for the water vault and lining it with rock and then using the bucket to fill it all back in again. We have dug trenches to put in culverts so the water runoff from the pastures will be diverted. We have used it to dig up pipe and lay water lines all over this place. I mean, that tractor is incredible and there is no way you can function out here without one.

Steve used that tractor and bucket to clear snow and then we got a rear blade so he could move more snow. I have several roads that I travel around our place to get hay, to dump manure, to feed horses and with a lot of snow it is not possible. Steve would spend up to four hours per day moving snow off my roads so I could function and do my animal chores. He would pick up snow and move it to a designated area that was out of the way and drag with the blade but this was long hard work. One year I looked out the window and that big powerful tractor was sliding on the icy road. Steve was having trouble steering because of the ice under the snow. Holy cow, this is not good. We called the local tire shop and asked about chains that would fit the tractor. Of course Steve had done the research. Regular chains would not work. He needed the ones with the aggressive cleats on them that weighed one hundred fifty pounds for each tire and cost $800.00 for the pair. I was not sure we needed something that expensive but Steve said that was what we needed. The tire shop had one set—no kidding, who bought that kind of chains? We got them and it took us all day to get them on right. We have to kind of hook them and then drive so the tractor does the work and rolls them on but then we have to adjust them and we have to have those bungee things (chain tensioners Steve tells me) so that they stayed tight. Of course Steve worked on them until they were perfect. I helped. I sat in the tractor and went forward and backward when he said to move. Anyway, that was another one of the very important things we bought. Steve has never had any trouble slipping on the ice since we got the chains and we live on small rolling hills. That tractor, with those chains is definitely a piece of impressive machinery. That year we pulled neighbors' cars out of the snow, out of the ditches and cleared roads so they could get out and we were able to do so much more because of those chains. I agreed that was money well spent if we were going to survive out here.

Near the last part of the winter that we had the most snow ever recorded, our great neighbor Garrett came over one snowy day and told us about his snow blower that hooks to the back of his tractor. He said we should come over, hook it up and try it out. Garrett is a delightful man. He makes me laugh, he owns most of this little valley but he is so kind and always shares everything and is the first guy to try to help solve any problem. He is truly one of the best people I have ever known. His wife Maralyse helps everyone. Together the two of them show so much initiative and desire to help so many people. I have truly never before met such sharing people. We have been very fortunate to buy our farm in a neighborhood with such delightful, helpful and fun people. Garrett will just stop by and ask if I have chocolate chip cookies. I make cookies and freeze the dough so when I need any cookies I just cut them off and cook them. Garrett will keep me laughing the whole time he is here. He has these wonderful stories and used to be an airline pilot and has these endless stories about everything. He has stopped asking me if I know where something is because he says of course you don't—which I don't. All we have done since we got here was work on making improvements to this place. We know our way to the local building suppliers, grocery store, feed store and the military base and that is about it.

Anyway, Garrett told us to try out his snow blower. What happened is he loved his tractor but it was not big enough for the things he needed to do so he went back to Jack and got a 90 horse power tractor with a cab with air conditioning and heater. Now that is a tractor. However, his current snow blower was now too small. We tried it out and instantly fell in love with it. With that snow blower Steve could clear the roads in one hour and did not have to go back and forth like before. He just drove and it chewed up snow and threw it out where he wanted it. Well, we bought the snow blower from Garrett and he got a newer, wider, heavier duty blower for a good deal because it did not work right but Garrett is so smart he fixed it in an hour and now helps all the neighbors when there is a heavy snow.

So, the best implements we have for the tractor are the forklift, auger, snow blower, backhoe and sometimes we use the cutter, the box scraper, the rear blade and we have a hopper type fertilizer spreader that is pretty cool but we do not use it all the time. That tractor does so many things. It allows us to live out here in the middle of nowhere.

I use my bright orange RTV every single day. It is amazing. It has four wheel drive that I use in the snow and the rainy muck. It has the rear bed that is a hydraulic dump. I use it to feed horses, to haul hay, to haul manure, to pull the drag to smooth the arena, to carry tools, to carry posts to fix the fences, to carry trash up the hill, to carry hoses or gardening supplies and to move the air conditioners from the building to the house and back. I have a few of my horses that I lead up and down the hill with the RTV. I drive the quarter mile down to the mail box to get mail each day. I honestly do not know how one could function out here without that RTV. It makes life so much easier. We even used it to help pull the electric wire that went to the water vault and had to come down to the well house. That distance is over four hundred yards. You would not think it would be a big deal to pull an electric wire through a pipe at that distance but even using wire lubrication we could not do it until Steve hooked the wire to the back of the RTV. Amazing.

We have used the RTV to herd cattle. During the summer when I have horses grazing I use it to go get them from up the hill. All the animals know when that RTV fires up at feeding time that dinner is coming. The cattle and the horses know that when I start the RTV in the middle of the day that I am going to make them move somewhere and the mares will start running down the hill before I get to them. In fact, the time the cattle got out, I got in the RTV and called them and they followed me right back up the hill to their pasture. We cut firewood and haul the cut wood back to the stacks. We take the trash up and down the hill. When we had to pull that calf, we used the RTV to brace one of the panels to keep the 1200 pound cow from pushing out. We carry gates, wood to build with and tools to do our work. That RTV is the absolute biggest workhorse on this place.

The only time I had a problem with the RTV was when we got over two feet of snow one night. The RTV could not get through or over that. Steve did clear my trails with the tractor and then I could use it. We did put chains on the back when we got the bad snow and ice and that helped a lot. I did slide a few times going up that hill before we got the chains but the chains solved any slipping problem. I use that RTV every single day and am lost without it.

Chapter 8

A SMALL CATASTROPHE

We had only been here for about a year but I noticed a moldy smell in the bathroom. I cleaned everything. I looked through the cupboards and could not find the problem. We finally checked the guest room and stepped on a squishy carpet. It turns out the back of the shower wall is up against the guest closet wall. The wall was totally moldy. Not good. We started pulling down wall board and found that there was a small leak with a very fine continuous spray coming from the water line. Thankfully, Steve can do anything and turned off the water to the house. We drove to town to get plugs for the lines. We came back, cut the water lines to the shower and plugged them and then Steve turned the water back on. We had to use the guest shower for a while. I called the insurance company and fortunately we had a good insurance company and they came right out. They sent a man out who evaluated the whole thing and gave us the number of a contractor who specialized in modular homes. While the insurance guy was here we said we had also noticed a problem with the water heater—that wall was also a little moldy. He said that if we made that claim also they would pay but would probably drop us so we did not submit that claim and tried to ignore that moldy wall. We had no idea the construction and standards were different for modular homes than they were for traditionally built homes. We called this contractor and he came out and wrote up an estimate. The insurance company approved the estimate and the contractor had it divided up into sections such as; wall, mold, pipes, paint, floor, carpet, etc. He said that Steve could work with him and anything we did we could be paid for that part of the job so we did some of the work ourselves but mostly Steve worked with the specialists and learned. We had to tear out the entire floor, the shower, the wall, the carpet and all that piping. It was quite a job but actually went quickly with the specialists. I have to say I was very impressed with our insurance company and the contractor he had recommended. It turns out that was a small job compared to the water heater.

Once we finished the whole shower wall job we opened the closet for the water heater. Oh my gosh. The floor was disintegrating and the water heater was tipped sideways and sinking into the floor. You have got to be kidding me. We closed it up and hoped it would last a while longer since the access to the water heater was outside and there was still snow on the ground. That night while Steve was watching TV he smelled something burning. He tried to track it down and turned off the electrical box where it seemed to be coming from. He went outside to the water heater door and opened it. It turns out the water heater had caught on fire but because it had tipped so far and was leaking water from the top the dripping water put out the fire. Holy cow. Again, we turned off the water and tried to evaluate what to do or what even happened. It turns out the previous owner had a leaky water heater so he had paid to have someone come out and install a new one and it looked great when we bought it—all new and nice. Well, what the installer did not notice was that modular homes have floors made of composite board and when it gets wet it disintegrates into saw dust. When the floor got wet the first time it started to disintegrate and the only thing holding the water heater up was a floor beam that was almost in the middle of the water heater.

Well, we needed a new water heater. However, we had to fix the floor first. We took out the old water heater and pulled out all the flooring. The mold was up both walls and the floor was nonexistent under the linoleum. We started following the water damage. It turns out we had to replace the water heater floor, the entire wash room floor, the closet floor, half of the kitchen floor and part of the family room floor before we got to sound wood. We had to take out cabinets, the refrigerator, the washer and dryer. We had to take out walls. The only good news in the whole thing was the fact that it had not damaged any of the major support beams. We had a problem with the refrigerator water dispenser leaking so we had shut that off when we first moved into the house. The problem was that the water heater had done so much damage to the floor that the refrigerator was only balanced on one beam and both sides were sunk into the floor but we did not realize that until we followed the damage from the water heater.

So, the washer and dryer were in the middle of the family room and not hooked up. The refrigerator was hooked up in the living room. There was no floor from the back door through the wash room and into the kitchen. We had no hot water. I had to boil water to get a 2 inch bath to try to get clean. A neighbor offered to let me shower at her house. Oh, my gosh, I got to wash my hair. We had to go to the Laundromat in town but that was not so bad, I could do all my loads of wash at one time once I figured out how to work the machines. The Laundromat lady yelled at me because I said the machine would not work and she showed me the error of my ways.

We worked on all of this for 4 months. Of course, Steve is a perfectionist and so very good at everything he does and he just works slowly. He had learned so much by working with the guys and the shower catastrophe. Steve beefed up the floor in the water heater room and painted it with this special rubberized paint so if it ever leaked again it would not penetrate the floor or the walls. He put in a new water heater with a special filter—that is cool. He beefed up the floors. I had not realized it but the back floor had disintegrated to the point that we could see dirt under the house but we had just lived with that. Gag me. It was never ending. Steve beefed up all the floors with blocking every foot. We tiled the floor and it is now really nice.

I finally got my house put back together and it was so nice to have hot water and a washing machine, a stable refrigerator, a wash room with no hole in the floor and really nice tile on a floor that did not sink when we walked on it.

We still have a leak in the sky light and now there is also a leak in the sky light in the bathroom. We have tarps over the top of both of those but they are not leaking at the moment. We do need a whole new roof but just one small catastrophe at a time.

Chapter 9

THE WATER VAULT

We have a very unique sixty foot deep hand dug well. Someone, a long time ago, chiseled through solid granite to make this well. It is six by six feet and we can see down to the bottom of this well. It is very impressive. However, we have to be careful about the water use. The second winter that we were here the temperatures were in the 20's for over a month. Well, the ground freezes hard and basically it slows down the water that comes into the well. We were almost out of water and it was not regenerating very fast. It is the middle of winter and we are running out of water—now what? I had enough water to flush toilets, take one shower a day and wash a load of clothes or do the dishes and trust me—we were thankful for that. We bought two 55 gallon barrels and drove a mile through the snow to our friend's house and they allowed us to fill up these tanks. They had a newer and deeper well that was not affected by this hard freeze. We would fill up the two 55 gallon tanks and then two six gallon tanks. We drove back and filled the horse tanks with the big barrels. We used the six gallon tanks to finish filling the washing machine or flush toilets. It was not fun but we were functioning in this really hard freeze.

We were at a loss. Do we put in a new well, what do we do? New wells are risky and they can cost $15,000 to $25,000 at the time depending on how deep we would have to drill the well. We did not have a lot of money. Our friends, Brian and Janie, are very smart. They had put in a vault system and Brian and Steve talked about how to do this. We figured we could put in a vault for around $5000 and function very well. We had to buy a back hoe for the tractor. That was not cheap but it was cheaper than a long term rental or paying someone else to dig it for us and plus we would use the back hoe for lots of other projects. After the ground thawed out we made our plan and started with the back hoe from the top of a hill to our well. Not a big deal—yeah right. That was at least four football fields away and one scoop at a time. We had to dig at least four feet deep so the new water line would not freeze. Steve used the back hoe until each section was right and then he got off, repositioned the tractor and then got back on to the backhoe part. When we finally trenched our way down the hill we had to assemble and glue the two inch pipe together and the electrical pipe and the air vent pipe. So we had three pipes and then we had to pull the electrical wire down the pipe for four football fields. I thought that was not a big deal but it is. We had to put this goop on the wire and Steve had very smartly built in these screw on openings so we could pull the wire 40 feet, pull it out and start over at that spot but we still had to hook the wire to the back of the RTV to pull the last 100 feet. Oh, so good we did not break it and have to start that over. We had ordered a concrete vault and Steve had to prepare the ground to put the vault into. It had to be totally flat to work right. You got it, we had to get a laser level but the vault is perfect and we have used the laser level on many other projects. It was October by the time we finished the whole thing. We had to fill in that big trench before winter hit. We decided not to hook it up because if there was a problem and the ground was already starting to freeze we would be in big trouble. So, we made it through the winter and then hooked the whole thing up the next spring.

This vault system is truly impressive. Our hand dug well pumps water up this two inch pipe to fill the vault. It is a three thousand gallon vault and we have a valve that works like the float in a toilet that is connected to the electrical wire we pulled. When the water level gets below the top 800 gallons the well pumps until it fills that and then quits until that is gone again. It really is a great idea. Even if the electricity goes out we have water because it comes down by gravity. This new system was much better for our pump because with the old system almost every time we flushed a toilet the well would come on because we only had a fifteen gallon holding tank in the pump room. A pump going on and off constantly is really hard on the pump. With the vault the well only comes on every couple days, pumps the 800 gallons and quits so this system is much better for the pump and we have water even if the electricity is out.

So, we have been here for three years. In that time we have fixed a vault system, torn apart half the house with the leaky shower and the burned out water heater and in the middle of all that the tax assessor says our house is worth $20,000 more than it was last year. I called and almost lost it. "How can this house possibly be worth that much more money when we have no water, the water heater fell through the floor and caught on fire, the shower wall has disintegrated, the guest bedroom is flooded, the walls have molded and we have no floor, no washer, no dryer and the sky light now leaks. How can this house possibly be worth more?" She very nicely said "well, I have a picture and it looks really nice." In my close to total breakdown mode she did agree there was a problem and left it as it was for that year.

Chapter 10

THE ELECTRIC FENCE

My brother Kym had come to visit in the spring. Out in front of the house we had four yearling horses, Tiffany, Aggie, Rock and Red in a fenced in area. Kym decided he wanted to walk out and be with them. I told him that the fence was electric but he was already in the process of climbing over the fence like all good cowboys. He swung a leg over the fence and as he put it on the board on the other side he had this strange look on his face and quickly got off the fence. I asked him if it zapped him and he grabbed his man hood and said now that was not an experience I would like to repeat and walked around a little strangely for a while. He did stay out there long enough to admire and talk to the horses.

Some of our electric fence chargers are more powerful than the others. Some just give a mild shock and let you know they are there and some feel like they can just stop your heart. I have had many encounters with the electric fences but one of the most memorable was the evening I was out feeding and I was wearing my glasses. It was just getting dark and I stuck my hand into the water tank to see how warm the water was because it was winter and there was steam coming off of the water and I thought it might be too hot. I thought I had been careful to avoid the electric wire but as I bent over to put my hand through the fence the wire hit my glasses, sending this huge spark into the air and scared the living day lights out of me besides giving me a headache. I was definitely impressed and wondered if I still had an eyebrow on that side and if I had done major brain damage. I thought I was probably ok if I knew the way down to dinner.

I did not want electric fences but it seems to be the only thing the horses really respect as far as fences go. Horses do not deal well with pain and will avoid the fences once they know the fence gives shocks. In fact, we have developed a very elaborate system of rotational grazing using a portable thin rope electric system that is held up by fiberglass step in stakes. We can move that system anywhere and the horses respect it and stay inside that area. We have put up a two inch wide electric tape across our driveway and just turn horses loose to graze around the house and they will not even mess with the tape. Once horses learn that the electric tape shocks them it does not matter if the tape is electrified or not. The horses will not try to push through it. This concept has allowed us to utilize a lot more of the property for grazing. In the spring we let horses out to graze everywhere. They are really pretty impressive. They graze the hill sides that are too hard to mow, edge around the house and just mow all the grass down so we do not have to do that extra work and it is wonderful green grass. This extra grazing around the house, barn and buildings allows our pasture grasses time to get more growth each spring before we let the horses on to start grazing on the new fields. It also cleans up all the extra grass around the buildings.

The electric fencing has given us so much versatility with the horses. We can allow them to graze every inch of the property using the portable fencing even if we do not have it hooked up. The horses respect the small rope fencing because they think it is electric and they will not mess with it. It truly is an amazing concept.

Chapter 11

SHE ADOPTED US—PUFF

*P*uff is a gorgeous tiger striped gray cat with white feet and a white bib. She is basically feral but does allow us to feed her and hug her once in a while.

It was our first year here and the beginning of winter. It was raining, cold but beautiful. I was reading my book by the window looking at the spectacular view when I heard this very unmistakable meow. I ignored it but it would not stop. I started looking out the window but I could not see where the noise was coming from. I put down my book and went out to the patio and looked around. I stood quietly and heard it again. I started calling and she talked back to me and was very obviously trying to tell me something. I tried to call her to come to me but she would have none of it. I walked into the house and got a handful of dog food and a little bit of milk. I shook the dog food and I could tell she was hungry but she was very leery of me. I set it down and backed away. She popped out from under the patio and watched me very carefully. I kept talking to her but she still kept her distance. I backed up some more and she very cautiously came to the food. She ate it all and looked at me. Oh, she was so beautiful—I named her Puff the Magic cat right there on the spot. She would not let me get close to her and left. The next day she was back and telling me that she was hungry. I fed her again. This went on daily for several weeks. She would not allow us to get close to her but she definitely came to tell me it was dinner time. We could not leave food out for her because there are coyotes, skunks and other critters that live out there and I did not want to draw them to the house. So, each night, after we came in from doing chores and brought the dogs inside I would wait for her to tell me it was dinner time. She had me trained so well. I bought her canned cat food and dry cat food—she seemed to like that better than dog food. She started letting me get closer but was still very cautious. I would sit on the bench on the front porch and put her food down closer to me each night. She started coming closer to eat but still shied away if I tried to pet her. One evening while I was sitting there she rubbed against my legs and then she let me pet her. Oh she was so beautiful and so grateful. As the winter got colder with more snow, I tried to get her into the house to eat in the wash room. She would have none of it but she still demanded her dinner. One night when it was very cold she came in to eat her dinner. I sat and talked to her and she let me pet her a bit but when she was finished eating she wanted out.

We got a low plastic box and put a soft cushion inside and put that on top of the dryer and got her a sand box with real kitty litter that we put on the floor. She would occasionally spend the night and looked so relaxed in her box. One day she left a dead mouse for me to find. She was so proud and I was excited the mouse was gone but grossed out. I went to get a plastic bag so I could pick it up but she had eaten it by the time I got back—gross but I guess that is better than leaving dead mice around. She would let me hold her and love her just for a little while. She got good at ignoring the dogs from her bed on the dryer as we let them out the back door to go to the bathroom. At first we had to stand in front of her so the dogs could go by but she learned they could not reach her so she just lay quietly in her box. When the heater came on she would start meowing very loudly until we let her out.

I always worried about her because I can hear the coyotes so close to the house. We have an owl that comes by occasionally and there are just a lot of predators out there. Puff got really good at knowing the routine. When we came in for the night and brought the dogs she would show up and start talking. If I was tired and did not want to wait for her I would go outside and call her and she would come from the barn or the hay storage up the hill. She talked the whole way and was so cute with her little white feet. She would run until she got close to me and then she would be very coy—what a crack up.

She would disappear for a few days and I would call for her but she did not come. I would worry and call but she came when she wanted to come by. She used to live on top of the hay in the barn but as the stack got smaller she was more threatened by the dogs so she would stay in the hay storage up the hill. When it rained really hard I am sure she could not hear me because the rain on the tin roofs is very loud.

Puff is a survivor. We are not sure where she came from but we think she came from a place a quarter of a mile away. Those people just moved out of that house one day. They were just gone. We never heard what happened but we did hear and basically saw the new owners cleaning out the place. The rumor was that their bottom room was filled with cats, food, scattered kitty litter and feces. It took them several trailer loads to just shovel that room out. I guess it was awful. It was sometime after the original people left that Puff showed up at our place. She must have been neutered because she has never had any kittens. There was another cat around and I tried to feed it also but it fought with Puff and drove her off so I only fed Puff in the house after that and she seemed relieved to be safe to eat her food.

The winter that we had 97 inches of snow—the all time, most snow ever for this area, I had not seen Puff for several days. The snow was so deep I was afraid she was stuck up at the hay barn. I walked up there and called her. She answered me back from somewhere in the hay. I kept calling and she kept answering and worked her way up to the front. I had to crawl under the tarp to get her. She does not like the snow. She seemed happy to see me and let me hug her and carry her down the hill. I fed her in the wash room but she hates the heater and started meowing loudly. I could not let her go out into that snow. She would be an easy target for predators because the snow was just too deep. We decided that we could put her in the tack room that has a refrigerator for horse carrots and extra sodas and a small heater that keeps that room from freezing but the heater is very quiet. We took all her stuff, her bed, her kitty litter, water and food out to the tack room. She was not happy but I could not let her go into that really deep snow. Even for Puff who is a master at getting away from the dogs it would be almost impossible for her to travel through several feet of snow. She had to stay in the tack room for the winter. After a while she got used to her cozy little room and would lay by the window in her very comfy box. When we walked in she would languidly roll over and look at us and stick out a paw—she was definitely the queen of her room. We kept her in food and water and loved her up every time we went in there. She would walk around and tell us she was not happy if we did not quickly change her liter box in the morning. She definitely has us trained well. When spring hit and the sun was bright and things warmed up she wanted out. We would let her out and sometimes she would demand to be let back in to her room and sometimes she would stay away for a few days.

Puff is definitely beautiful, smart, demanding and truly a survivor. We forget she is basically feral because she is nice to us and seems to like us. Any time we have company she disappears until the company leaves and then she shows back up wanting to be fed. She is definitely part of this huge menagerie of ours. We love her but allow her to do what she wants most of the time. For a while she was catching birds at our bird feeder. She is a pretty good hunter but I did not think that was fair. We watched her and figured out where she was hiding. We had left a piece of plywood leaning up against the well house and she would sit quietly between the plywood and the well house and jump out and grab birds that picked up seed off the ground. We moved the plywood and that seemed to stop the bird catching, at least the ones we knew about.

Puff is now getting pretty old. We have no idea how old she truly is but she was full grown when she adopted us and we have now been here for seven years. I am pretty impressed that she still seems to be able to hold her own out there when she leaves for days at a time.

I would love to keep her safe in the tack room but I realize that she was feral when she came and loves to be out there, hunting and free to do what she wants. She has started to get a little more particular. When we go into her tack room in the morning sometimes she times the door and comes out. She will walk around, test out the temperature on the cement floor, look at the snow or the rain or whatever and then sometimes she just demands to be back inside and sometimes she just wanders off to do whatever she wants. I worry but I guess it is like kids, at some point you have to let them go and test the world. So far she has always come back. Sometimes she is thin and will stay for several days and sleep and eat and just kick back but then she is ready to go out there again. I surely love that wild spirit and enjoy the fact that she trusts us enough to let us hold her and love her up.

Chapter 12

THE MOST SNOW EVER

I love the snow. It is beautiful and the cool air is so refreshing. I could sit in the house and watch it snow in big, fat flakes and feel like I was part of a snow globe. It made the mountains and trees and ground all look so clean and beautiful. What did I know; I was a southern California girl. My mom once told me that if it ever snowed we could stay home from school. I was so excited but it never snowed where we lived.

This particular year we got the most snow ever in the recorded history of the area. We got 97.7 inches of snow. It was incredible and it just never seemed to stop. I went to bed one night and got up with two feet of snow on the ground. My RTV could not get up the hill to feed the horses—there was just too much snow and it could not get up on top of it so it just plowed right into it and could go no further. I had to shovel out in front of the barn to even try to get out. That was the time I used the snow shovel and piled it high with flakes of alfalfa, tied them on and dragged it up the hill to feed. I had to wade through this soft, gorgeous powder that was up to my knees. That took me several trips but I did get them fed. Next I had to find the hoses that were somewhere under the snow because we had them draining down the hill, hook them together and drag them up the hill to fill the water tanks after I broke the ice in the hundred gallon tanks. Then I had to disconnect them and put them where I could find them so they would drain down the hill. If they froze, the water would not go through and I would have to drag the hose into the warm tack room, roll it up in this big bucket so the ice inside would melt and then drag out another hose to take its place. After I got the horses fed, I started looking at the buildings. They also had two plus feet of snow on top of them. We had been watching the news and they said we should shovel off anything that got that deep so the building did not collapse. Steve started working on the trails so I could use the RTV to feed. At that time we did not have the snow blower so he just used the bucket, pushed it into a pile and then picked up snow and stacked it off the road—back and forth, back and forth, endless. While he was doing that I started shoveling off the roof. We live in a double wide modular home with an almost flat roof. It has twenty-five vents and pipes and two skylights and a television dish and with that much snow I cannot see them so I have to shovel carefully. First, I have to get up there. We set a ladder by the roof in the winter that gets frozen into that spot and actually becomes pretty stable. However, I do have to get from the ladder onto the roof. I basically crawl. I am an old lady and I try to keep my body intact. Steve says I cannot wear my cleats up there but I say would you rather have me slide off—who would make you dinner and then you would have to feed the animals in the morning. He lets me wear the cleats and I am careful. Where do you start with that much snow? I guess I will try the edges; I will not have to throw the snow that far. Another lesson to learn; wet snow sticks to shovels. Steve gets me a can of spray oil. I spray it on the shovel, front and back, and then I can shovel for ten plus minutes. This is all part of the free gym membership that came with this place. Each shovel of snow weighs about fifteen pounds so if I lift that and toss it a thousand plus times I am sure working several muscle groups and I don't even have to join a gym. It takes me three plus hours to do most of it and then Steve comes up to help. It takes forever but at least I will be able to sleep tonight knowing the roof won't collapse because of the snow load. It snows again and again and I shovel the roof three times that winter. I got better and I got faster—you know the free gym membership I was getting stronger. We had some trees growing by the house and when I tried to throw snow it hit the trees and fell back onto the roof. The only thing worse than having to shovel was having to shovel the same stuff twice. I decided to cut those trees down below the roof. Ha—how can you even get to them because the snow is too deep? I use my brilliant brain and open the window, take off the screen, clip the trees and let the branches fall where they fall. That summer we took those trees down. Oh yeah!!

I now know how people die in the deep snow. We tried to walk on a deer trail in the forest. If I stepped off the trail or leaned, there is nothing to catch. I cannot push myself up with my hands because my hands do not touch anything solid and my face goes into the snow. If I can get turned over I just wallow around in it until I can get some kind of footing or Steve helps me up—downright scary—we stay out of the forest this winter.

We heard on the news that forty commercial buildings down town have collapsed because of the snow and they are not even keeping track of the individual homes or small out buildings. We see several collapsed buildings and sheds on our way to town. We hear that a horse shelter down the road collapsed and killed one of their horses. I cannot even imagine how sad that was.

We had a total of nine buildings counting house, barn and the sheds and shelters. Each day we try to figure out which one is in the most danger of collapsing and spend the day trying to get snow off of it. We bought this great tool. It is a scraper with an extended handled. It reaches way up and I drag snow off—that is only if it is not frozen and then it does not work at all. It works great in the soft, fresh powder. Most of our out buildings have metal roofs which is awesome because the snow usually slides off when it gets heavy but I cannot walk on them because they are too slippery. Well, this year, nothing is sliding. I guess it melted a bit and then froze for that bottom layer and nothing is moving. We take the most valuable tool on the place, the tractor, and we take turns lifting each other up on the platform so we can shovel and pull snow off the buildings. Every day for a solid three weeks we shovel and move snow and it just keeps snowing. Where do we even put that much snow? We just stacked it out of the way. The horses had trails that they made from the shelter to the food and the water. They are actually very smart. They pooped all along these trails so the footing is not slippery and their weight mashes it down. They walk the same trails every day and keep it open. The horses that are in the barn with run outs poop, it snows and covers it, freeze, poop, snows and covers it. Holy cow. You cannot shovel it up because it freezes and unless you chip each piece out, it does not work. I can see the layers of poop and snow—amazing. I keep their inside stalls clean everyday but I can do nothing with the outside until spring. Now that is ugly when it melts and the poop piles up on the ground. I had to make trails so the horses could get out their doors. I had to cut into the four feet of snow so they could go in and out. I had to chip the snow hanging off the roof so there was room to walk out. I was sure the horses were just going to walk right over the fence because there was so much snow. Each stall was like a frozen cocoon. Each stall was a nice twelve by twelve foot area with snow hanging off the roof, snow on the ground and only the single small trail through the middle of it to get to the outside run out. It was amazing.

In the middle of all the constant shoveling neighbors would call and say they slipped off the road. Steve would go and pull them out with the tractor. One of the neighbors had a snow plow on the front of his truck and went off the side of the road and into the ditch which he could not see. Steve pulled him out. It was just this constant effort to try to survive out here. Shovel snow and clear the buildings, feed and water the animals, eat and fall into bed and get up to start over. We were snowed in for several days. That was not a big deal; we keep food stored just because it is so far to go to town. I did not mind being snowed in and this was a huge adventure—woman against nature. I still love the snow.

We have the foundation to an old building behind our house. We could not even get to it because the snow was too high and it collapsed. We still have not had time to deal with that. It was a one room, rock and cement house with huge, strong trees holding up the ceiling. It was sad to see it go down but we were still in survival mode and saving that building was not a high priority.

I had a doctor's appointment and I called to cancel it. I told the secretary I would reschedule when our animals and buildings were safe. She told me I could die if I did not get my blood test. I told her I could die if my roof collapsed on my head and further more we were snowed in and could not get to the road. She wanted me to come anyway. Obviously, some people have no idea what it is like to live in the country on dirt roads with nobody plowing the roads except us and we were still trying to survive. She actually got mad at me—are you kidding me I cannot even get the truck out much less drive through four feet of snow by now—I guess I will just have to take my chances. She did not like that.

I have to admit it was incredibly beautiful with all this snow. I would take breaks while shoveling off the roof and just look at the spectacular view. Were we lucky or what? Back to shoveling.

It did finally stop snowing and we were able to dig out and I did reschedule my appointment and we did survive but wow, how did people live out here before there was electricity. Amazing.

Chapter 13

JOSIE—SO TOUGH TO DEAL WITH

We had gotten our horses Josie and Blue from a lady that was having a hard time feeding her horses. Josie was three years old and Blue was just a year old gelding. We also got Dancer who was also a year old gelding and a half brother to Tiffany. Josie and Blue can both be registered as Kentucky Mountain horses and Dancer is registered as both Kentucky Mountain and Rocky Mountain so they were all the same breed as our horses.

Josie and Blue were so thin we could see their ribs and their hips stuck out. We were so happy to have them both. It took them an hour and a half to catch Blue at the lady's house because he was so wild. Now, we cannot get away from Blue. He always wants to be where we are. He goes through my pockets, chews the handle of the rake when I am trying to clean stalls and follows me everywhere. He is just so cute and friendly. He is black with three white feet and a white blaze on his face.

Josie is just so perfect. She is all black with a very refined head, thick black mane and tail and so high stepping and incredibly beautiful and proud but also very wild. She is special. We think all our horses are beautiful but Josie is very striking and so fancy.

It was the end of January and we had already had four of our twelve horses colic with only one of those having to go to the vet to be treated. There are three types of colic: impaction, sand or in extreme cases a twist in the intestine. Horses do not do well with any kind of pain and can become self destructive. We are not sure why we had so many horses colic this year. It may have been the food or it may have been because we had so little snow and a lot of rain and the horses were getting dirt with their food.

I am the one that loves and is fascinated by the horses. Steve always helps me with whatever I need but I am the one that watches them daily, feeds them, cleans their stalls, brushes them and mostly I ride every day. I know when one of the horses is not feeling well or has a cut or needs to have their feet trimmed and filed.

Josie did not feel well. She was lying down too much and just not herself. I brought her down to the barn with Blue and Dancer because horses hate to be alone. They need to be part of a herd. Josie was not happy being in a stall and she paced and whinnied and it just tugged at my heart because it was just awful to watch because she was so unhappy. We had to put her in a stall by herself so we could watch to see if she pooped. A horse can poop up to 50 pounds of poop per day and will poop every couple hours. Watching the quantity of poop is one of the good indicators of how the horse is doing. We can also watch water consumption when we have them isolated. That night she did have one normal volume poop—not good but at least a poop. We put her out with Blue and Dancer with food but she ate a little, wondered around and then just laid down in the food. This was definitely not good. We brought her in, took away all her food, checked all her vital signs which were ok but not great and we kept an eye on her all day. We called the vet and he said to give her banamine, kind of a horse aspirin, relaxant.

The next morning she did have a few poops, looked better but she was not drinking water. We gave her a handful of hay; she would not eat, just kept pacing and lying down. We took her to the vet. He put a tube down her nose that goes to the stomach and pumped in a whole lot of mineral oil and gave her banamine. We brought her back home and checked her every two hours. She did push out some of the oil but no poop and we did not feed her. If there is a blockage we do not want to compound it by adding more food to the blockage so she got no food and would not drink her water. Each time we checked all night long, there was oil but no poop and she still was not drinking.

The next morning just a couple small poops. She was still not drinking any water. We walked her up to her own water tank but she still would not drink. Josie is now down and shaking. We took her back to the vet. They did a rectal exam and tubed her again with psillium and gave her two and three quarter gallons of water through the tube. We took her home. We took her for short walks. She clearly does not feel well. She is kicking at her stomach, has oil oozing down her tail and all over her back legs but no poop. Again, we check her every couple hours all night and take her for short walks. She is getting Banamine shots to help relax and relieve the pain. She is now laying in the oil and some pee but she is still not drinking. Steve walks her and I clean out the stall.

Back to the vet the next day, more oil and more water. She has now gone several days and she is not pooping and she is not drinking. She is getting weaker and quieter. She does not want to be petted, brushed or anything. She does quietly walk with us for short walks to try to help her whole body. The vet can feel a cantaloupe size soft obstruction when he does a pelvic exam.

Again, we watch her all night. We take turns taking her for short walks while the other person cleans the stall. She is lethargic but walks with us. She seems to know that we are trying to help but she looks as if she feels so awful.

She is getting weaker and just looks so pathetic with oil on her tail and legs, pee on her side where she has laid in it but she does not want to be touched. She tolerates us but does not seem to care. We went back to the vet. They do another rectal exam, the lump is still there but they do pull out two huge handfuls of black sand. The vet tells me that this sand is not from around here. I feel better that maybe I have not caused all of this. He says that horses can get 20 to 30 pounds of sand that they carry around in their gut until they get a blockage like this. I am in tears and I tell the vet that I hate to watch her in such pain and if he thinks we cannot save her then just put her down. We are getting no sleep which is Ok but I want to save this beautiful animal and this is just so painful to watch this proud, beautiful horse disintegrate in front of my eyes. They say for us to leave her there but I tell them that there is nothing they can do for her that we cannot do for her and she trusts us. We would rather bring her back every day. We check her and walk her every couple hours. They give her psillium again and two gallons of water and they give her three one and a half liter IV bags of fluid.

This whole tragic, sad series of events continues for eight days. She does not drink and she does not poop. Each day we take her to the vet and they give oil or psillium and do a rectal exam. Each day they pull out handfuls of this black sand. The only fluid she is getting is what they put in. Every day she gets shots of banamine to help with the pain but the vet warns that sometimes you can get abscesses from the banamine shots so now I start to look for that also. She finally poops out this huge pile of black sand and then she starts to poop. How can she possibly poop when she has had no food for eight days but she does. Her system is starting to work. We have turned the corner. The next day, she cannot bend down to eat the small amount of food we have started to give her. She has her legs splayed and is trying to get her head down. I feel her neck, there is a huge knot. I tell Steve she is getting an abscess and it is a football playoff day and he says let's wait until tomorrow. I say no, this is an abscess and by tomorrow it will be worse. She needs antibiotics now. We call the vet and he says bring her down because he is already at the office because another horse with the same problem is coming in to the office. We get there and this other beautiful buckskin horse's neck is so swollen it is solid and it cannot move. It just stands there in absolute pain. The people could not get that horse in the trailer the day before so they had waited an extra day. I am so thankful I insisted we bring Josie in this day.

The vet takes time from that other horse and gives Josie a shot of penicillin and we are supposed to give her penicillin twice a day for 5 days. Josie is now starting to eat, starting to drink and is definitely getting better. The abscess is now the size of a large golf ball and it is oozing and looks awful. I ask the vet if we should be doing anything else and he says no, the antibiotic will wall off the abscess and it will probably break on its own. Josie can no longer stand the shots. We go back and get the rest of the antibiotic in pill form. We complete the series of penicillin. Josie rolls and breaks open the abscess. We clean it with betadyne and put nolvasan ointment on it. When the abscess finally broke it was the size of a tennis ball. We had to go back to the vet to get the nolvasan and even he was impressed with the size of the abscess.

Josie did start to eat and drink but she looked like a walking scare crow. She lost the hair on the back of her legs because of all the oil and psillium. She had the big scar on her neck and just looked awful but her spirit was coming back.

Josie has filled in the abscess scar with hair, the hair has grown back on her legs and she has put on weight and has regained her spirit and she is the incredibly beautiful horse that she was before this whole ordeal started. We are fortunate that we never had a problem getting her into the trailer or taking her medicine or having the vets work on her. She is not as wild as she was before the colic and seems to trust us more. It all started on January 27 and the last journal entry of medication I have is on the 25th of February. Wow, I feel we were so fortunate and I am thankful every day to have Josie out there with the other horses and so thankful that we have vets that can help and know what to do.

I was so worried about the other buckskin horse that I had to ask the vet what happened because I was so sad for him and for his owners. The vet said that he had been there for a week and had a very rough time but he did make it and he did get to go home. That made me happy.

Chapter 14

THE TURKEYS

We have a bird feeder that hangs off the well-house and we watch it through the kitchen window and from the computer in the family room. We get all kinds of birds all year long and they are delightful to watch. We have wood peckers that peck at the well house and hang upside down to eat the suet. We get dove, pheasant, red wing black birds, bright yellow birds, robins, blue birds, turkeys and many more. In the winter time we have had turkeys walk up to the ground beneath the feeder to eat the food that was dropped by the other birds. These turkeys are huge and they walk everywhere. They only fly when they are in absolute danger of being caught. We come across them in the forest, in the pastures and at the bird feeder. They are a crack up to watch. If I have the dogs with me the turkeys will walk as fast as they can until the dogs get to within about five feet and then they will take off and fly. They are huge and cumbersome but they do fly well.

The most turkeys we ever had was thirty-three that just kept coming to the bird feeder. They walked up the driveway, across the snow-covered lawn and right up to the bird feeder. They were busy scratching in the snow to uncover any snow covered sunflower seeds. When the winters are really hard we also throw out cracked corn for them and they love it. We had a group that made it a daily event to walk up to scratch for food and then they walked up the hill and were gone.

On this particular day Kym, my brother, and Jessie his daughter were here visiting and we had gone for a long walk on the back of our property. The five Labradors went with us. They love to go for these walks. The back of the property is pretty wild and there are not clear trails except for what the deer make so we usually follow the deer trails. There are downed trees, lots of shrubs, lots of gulleys and up and down hills. It is pretty wild back there. We will come across animal parts that have either just died or something killed it and the coyotes and crows have cleaned it up except for a few bones and even those are scattered all over.

We were having a delightful walk and the dogs were checking out everything. All of a sudden there were these crashing sounds as the dogs found a turkey that was hiding in the shrubs. The dogs went after the turkey and it could not seem to get away because of the five dogs and all the shrubbery. They crashed through the trees and bushes and went twenty feet down the hill in a big pile of dogs and turkey with Kym following as quickly as he could. He waded into the middle of the melee and I called the dogs and somehow we got them separated and that turkey had just the moment to get away from dogs and bushes and it took off flying through the trees and away from the dogs. We were all pleased, especially Kym, that he had saved the turkey. The dogs seemed pleased that they had found the turkey and continued to look for more. They are not mean dogs but they are bird dogs and it is natural for them to want to catch and retrieve any type of bird.

Chapter 15

MY BIGGEST FALL

*I*t was the middle of winter and very cold outside. There was about two feet of snow on the ground but Steve had cleared off the roads that I used to take food to the animals. We have a twelve by twelve foot bay in the barn that we keep filled with hay so that I can load up each meal for all the animals into the back of my RTV while I am in the protection of the barn regardless of what the weather is doing outside. The barn protects me from rain or snow but it is still almost as cold as outside.

I was loading alfalfa bales that weigh about eighty to one hundred pounds each and are packed tightly together so they are sometimes hard to pull out. I park my RTV close to the alfalfa so I do not have to carry the bale very far. I was cold and it was early and the horses were hungry. I was pulling hard on this bale but it would not budge. I thought I had it hooked with my hay hook so that it was through the hay and the baling twine. I planted both feet and gave one last massive pull and the hook pulled out of the bale because it was obviously not hooked on the twine and I went flying backwards. I had been standing on the bottom row of hay where I can slip between bales if they are not packed tightly. I landed on my butt on that bottom row of bales and slammed backwards against the bumper of the RTV. My back hit the RTV hard and my head snapped back and hit the side of the fender. Oh my gosh, I could not breathe, my back was killing me and I thought I was paralyzed from the waist down. I was wedged between that bottom row of bales and the RTV. I sat there and tried to catch my breath and thought how stupid this whole thing was. Of all the ways I could get hurt out here this was really dumb. When I could finally breathe I wiggled my hands and they worked I tried my feet and they worked and I could breathe but my back was killing me. I was so thankful I was not paralyzed but I was definitely hurt. I knew the horses were hungry and all the animals had to be fed. I crawled back onto my feet and very carefully hooked the bale by the string. I stood sideways so I would not fall pulling the bale out. I did finally get it out, loaded it and got another bale. I started the RTV and went to feed all the horses and fill the water buckets. I was crying the whole time. I gave the cat food and water and emptied her liter box. I went back into the house, still in tears but oh so glad that I had not permanently damaged myself. I got little sympathy from Steve but basically, I do not give him much sympathy when he gets hurt. I was sore for months but just happy I had not done major damage.

Out here, there are things that just have to be done. It does not matter what the weather looks like, rain, snow, wind, hail or whatever, the animals have to be fed on schedule. It does not matter if we are sick or want to sleep in for a while. The animals have to be fed. They do not care if it is Christmas or Sunday or any special day—they are on a schedule and it cannot be changed. You can make it a little earlier or a little later but the schedule is important. If we really had a problem we could call a neighbor to help but they are just as busy as we are and then they would have to go home and do their own chores. So, unless we are in the hospital, there is no calling in sick. In fact, when I had my surgery at seven in the morning Steve said he would be there. I told him that was stupid because there is nothing he could do for me while I was in surgery. I told him to sleep in, do the morning chores and then come see me. Hopefully, by then I would be out of surgery and he would not waste his whole morning waiting for me. If I died, I loved him but I would rather have the animals fed and come see me later when I could actually talk and was awake. So, that is what he did. I think it was much less stressful for him because he was not sitting in the waiting room for hours and he got to sleep in at our own house and in our own bed.

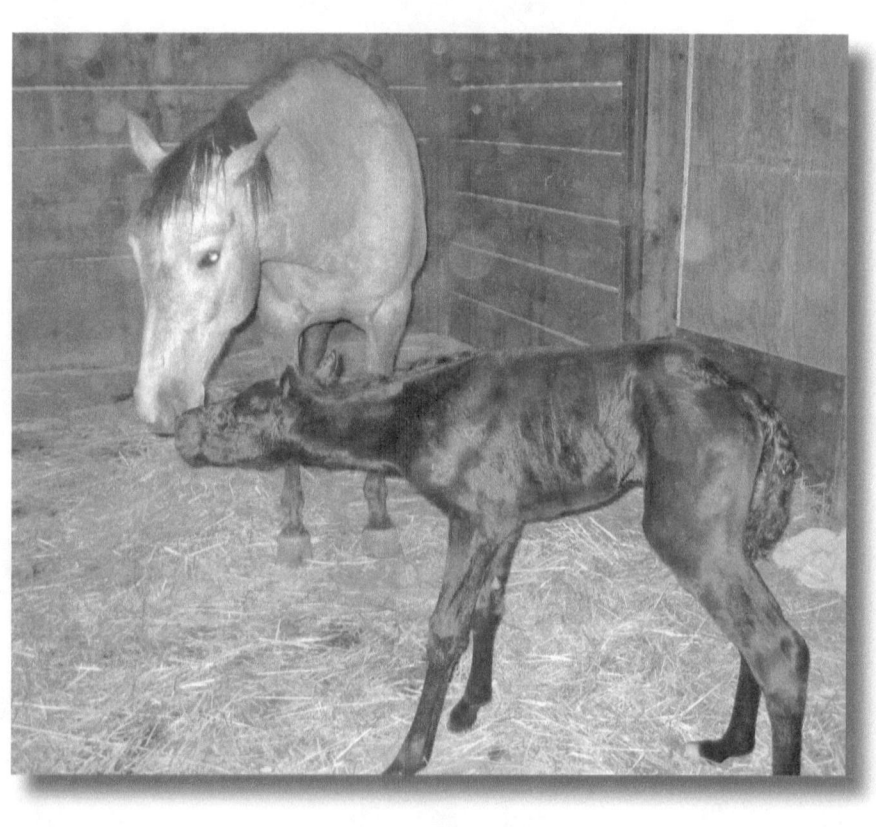

Chapter 16

FLAT OUT GORGEOUS—FOG

*H*er name is FOG—short for Flat out Gorgeous. She is the first and only horse to be born at our place. We sent Aggie and Tiffany to our trainer who had this amazing black and white spotted mountain horse with a wonderful gait. Aggie got pregnant and Tiffany did not.

Horses are pregnant for eleven months and for most of that time Aggie did not even look like she was pregnant. Aggie started out as a black horse when we got her as a yearling but each year she filled in with more gray. Now she has a black mane, black tail, black legs and the rest is gray. She is double registered as Rocky Mountain and Kentucky Mountain gaited horses. Our trainer said she was so funny when they went to breed her. He said she parked herself near the stallion and would not move. They had to bring the stallion to her.

About the last month of pregnancy Aggie started to get fatter and slower and take more naps. We watched her carefully and never went anywhere for very long. We went to our neighbors for dinner and got home around nine at night. I told Steve to check Aggie while I let the dogs out. Steve hollered at me and said, "If you want to see this baby born, you better come now." Oh my gosh. We had read books, watched videos and got all the stuff they said we needed. We were so nervous.

Steve found Aggie outside lying down and a foal's foot starting to come out. He put a halter on Aggie and got her to come inside to the double stall with nice straw that we had fixed up for her. She casually walked inside and then lay back down. I called our trainer who very kindly stayed on the phone for the whole process since we have never had a baby foal before. Pretty soon we saw two little hooves and they were front feet—that is good. Aggie pushed and Fog started to just slide right out. There was lots of water, a little blood and this sack still on her. Steve moved the sack away from her nose and pulled it back and helped her get out of the sack. Steve dried her off and rubbed her everywhere. That is called imprinting. Aggie stood up and began to lick little Fog.

Fog was born at 9:35 PM

Fog is up and wobbly at 9:55

Fog is walking around 10:15

Fog went round and round in this 24 by 12 foot stall. She was gaiting everywhere by 10:30

Aggie drops the rest of the placenta at 11:10

Fog nurses and lays down for a nap

After we watched and saw Fog nurse and Aggie drop the rest of the after birth, we cleaned up the straw, fed Aggie and we went to bed. We were excited, pleased and thankful that Fog was ok and that we had no problems.

We took the afterbirth to the vet so he could check to see that it was all there and there was no retained afterbirth that could cause problems.

We kept Fog and Aggie inside for the next day and the second day we let them out. Tiffany was in the stall next to Aggie to keep her company before the birth. When Fog and Aggie came outside Tiffany bared her teeth and pinned her ears back at this new little thing but Aggie always stayed between the two of them.

Little Fog is darling and quickly learned the routines. She tried to kick at me twice but missed me both times. I asked the trainer and he said he always came up to them on the side, never giving them that chance to kick at you.

We got a little halter for Fog and it was always easy to put on her. She is smart, beautiful and now at three years old she is turning a little grayer each year. Because this breed of horse matures late we will not ride her until she is almost four years old. She is just three this year.

We basically touch, pet and just talk to Fog. She is not a problem to trim her feet or brush her or lead her around with a halter. We have a cross tie that is just outside the girls area and when the farrier comes Fog watches and just steps up for her turn. She is a little head strong and independent but really a gorgeous horse. The farrier is impressed with her legs, body and build.

Chapter 17

THE CATTLE

We had thought about getting cattle since the day we got here but we had been so busy there was just not time. The whole process was not by total design. We did not have the time or the money to build the fences to keep cattle inside the property and the smooth wire fences we had with rotten wood posts just would not hold cattle if they wanted out.

During the worst snow year ever a couple had bought a five acre piece of property that borders our forest and put their truck with camper on it. At that time it became apparent that we had no idea where the property line was so if they started building we could not say if they were on our property or not so that spring we paid a surveyor to survey that side of the property and install four marker posts. Of course by that time the people had left because there was no way they could survive that winter without electricity, water or anything. They could not even move their truck much less get a car back there.

The surveyor came and marked our property with the four stakes. Wow, we had no idea that the property line was way over there. We gained about thirty more yards all the way down that side. When we looked back on it that made sense because someone had totally logged their property and that was the edge of our big trees. We had asked the previous owner where the property line was and he said about here. When I pushed him for more details he said what does it matter, there is no one out here. You gotta love it. Well, since the truck with the camper was gone we did not fence that side.

I think a year went by and then just before hunting season three guys in a truck showed up with maps, tree stands and all kinds of stuff. The neighbors across the road were putting a second trailer on their property so with the hunters, the trailers and all the commotion I stopped on my way to the mail box in my RTV. It turns out that there are two five acre parcels that border that side of our property. The hunters were the guys that owned that front five acres that still had trees. I asked them what they were doing. They said they were going to hunt. I said "on five acres, where are you going to shoot because there are houses on all four sides and I also have horses right over there." They said, "oh, we are just bow hunters and there is a ten acre piece right here." I said "Yes, I know, it belongs to us." At this point they asked if they could hunt on it and I said no because we have horses right there. Well, at that point they were no longer interested in us. I did point out the edge of the property that was now marked with a survey post and told them at some point we were going to put cattle in there but it probably would not happen this year. You have got to be kidding me. The very next day I was riding my horse out there and they had put up a deer stand just ten feet from our property line and facing into our property and put out salt blocks with molasses right on our property. Now, can you tell me where they were going to shoot—right toward our house? Steve and I talked about it and decided that we could no longer put this off, we had to put up that fence since clearly they were going to hunt our land and shoot toward our house and horses and try to lure the deer into their area.

Our friends who own cattle have two neighbor kids that they have known forever. Josh and Joe are two of the absolute nicest kids out there. They know how to work hard, they know how to put up fence and they are a lot younger and stronger than we are. We hired them to come put up fence that week. We bought all the barbed wire, t-posts and rail road ties we would need to put up the fence separating our properties. Now, of course this forest has been wild for ever so we would have to knock down brush, take down trees in the way along the property line and hand pound all these posts. Josh and Joe showed up on time and ready to work. We had the RTV loaded with tools and Steve loaded up the tractor with t-posts and off we went to the forest. Holy cow. Not only are these kids nice and polite but they are working machines. We kind of worked with them, I drove the RTV with the tools and kept them company and saw to it that they had the things they needed and carried the water and snacks in the RTV. Steve did a lot more of the work with the posts and set up.

I had always felt that the twine from the hay bales was wasted and had a use so when I cut the twine off the bales I tied them end to end and got the plastic rolls from wire from a home improvement store and just rolled it up. I had several hundred feet of the twine on several rolls. We took that twine and stretched it from marker to marker. It actually worked really well because if we had gone around a tree the wrong side it was easy to see the change in the line and we just untied the twine and tied it on the other side of the tree. I used my great geometry to show that "between any two points there is only one line." So we knew we were right on the property line. We had to cut down a few small trees that were right on the line but we got it stretched out straight from the front through the two middle markers and all the way to the end. Josh and Joe had to cut, pull or chop down anything that was on that line. There were a few areas that took a while to clear out. Josh and Joe said we had to stretch the wire before we could put up the posts. I think they were right because we have one of the nicest four strand barbed wire fences in the neighborhood. Anyway, they got up that entire side of the fence in two or three days with four strands of barbed wire. They also knew that anytime we went up a hill or there was a big change in height we had to put in a railroad tie or the T-post would eventually work its way out, so we did that. We had thrown the salt blocks over the fence and off our property. I am not sure what the hunters had to say but even I was impressed we got the fence up so fast.

We own two ten acre parcels running next to each other. Josh and Joe helped us fence it so it was divided into two separate areas that we call cow 1 and cow 2 so we can do rotational grazing out there. We put a gate in between so we could run the cattle from one pasture to the next. Steve built these incredible feed bunkers that we could put two bales of hay in each and corn and sunflower seeds. It was way cool.

Of course at the same time we were working on this whole thing I also thought we needed chickens—as if we did not have enough to do. So, we were trying to fix the cattle area and the chicken stuff—what was I thinking.

I had asked our friends with cattle if we could just buy cattle from them but they said they were growing theirs for market and we should go to the auction. Oh my. We drove our little car to the auction and just watched the first time we went. Oh boy, they brought cattle in, they were weighed on the scale and the auctioneer was calling out these bids. Well, some cattle they sold by dollars amounts as a whole animal and some were being sold by the pound. How the heck do you figure that out and it was all going so fast. They brought in groups of varying quantities of cattle. There is no way I can buy ten cows. I kept watching and listening and watching the weights. It turns out the young calves if sold by themselves are sold by dollar amounts, the cow/calf pairs and the bulls were also sold by dollar amounts as individual units with bidding setting the price. Most everything else was sold by so much per pound so I had to figure out how much that would be in dollars before I could even think about bidding. It was all very fascinating, fast and scary. The first time we just watched. I started to figure out the whole process but still had trouble figuring out who was bidding. I realized that a fifty cent cow that weighed about a thousand pounds would cost about five hundred dollars so I started getting faster and better at figuring it out.

The second time we went we pulled the trailer and we were ready to buy a cow/calf pair. That is a cow that already has this year's calf on the ground and we can see if we like them or not. I am not sure what I should be looking at but at least I had a feeling for how it all went. They kept running these big groups through that would cost thousands of dollars and we did not have enough room for them. I knew I wanted Black Angus. A group of two Black Angus cows with calves came in and by the time I hit my friend and said "that looks good, what do you think," they were sold. I had to get better at this. A single big Black Angus cow with a great looking calf came into the ring. I wanted that pair. They were selling by the dollar and they started at $1200. My friend said just wait, they are not getting any bids for that. I waited and when they started bidding I was on the edge of my seat. The auctioneer said a price and I raised my whole arm, nothing shy about me. I never even saw anyone else bid for anything. The auctioneer pointed in some direction and I raised my hand again. I just kept raising my hand until my friend said, stop, you are the only one bidding and they had watched the auctioneer and I did not bid against myself. Oh boy, I just bought a cow and a calf—holy crap, now what? Are they healthy, was that a good deal, where will they put them so no one else gets them? I was proud but so nervous. We did get a good price. I waited and watched and pretty soon a white faced black cow came in with a calf. I liked her; she was young and looked good. I waited until someone started bidding and again I was on the edge of my seat, throwing my arm in the air. My friends were laughing at me and I am sure everyone in the auction knew I wanted that cow/calf pair. I got almost the exact same price for these two and my friends had to tell me when to stop bidding because every time he said something I bid again—I do not think I am good at this. Oh boy. Now I have two cow/calf pairs. Oh boy, am I nervous. I was so excited. We were now big ranchers. Ha!! I am so clueless; we had not even finished our cattle pasture yet. We went back and turned in our paper work and paid and got our papers. We took that to the back, brought up the trailer and they loaded them into the trailer. I had to look closely to make sure those were my cows.

On the way home we had to stop on the two lane road because there was a jack knifed big rig so the calves were named Delay and Road Block. The moms were named Midnight for the all black one and White Face for the black one with the white face.

We brought them all home and unloaded them at Tom and Donna's because our pen was not finished. Tom and Donna also had a chute and a squeeze with a header so we could give them shots and tag their ears. We went over morning and night to feed our herd and check on them.

I decided that we did not want to have open cows, unbred cows, over winter so we needed a bull. Two weeks later we went back to the auction. I wanted a Black Angus bull. They finally brought in this group of three bulls. I did not need three bulls. I guess the bidding was not going the way they wanted so they said total dollars and high bidder gets first pick. I was back in the game and kept raising my hand until my friends told me to stop. The auctioneer asked which one I wanted and my friends helped me tell them which one. Oh boy, he was cheaper than the cow/calf pairs and he was so good looking. He had a big head, a powerful neck and was quiet. I named him Manly. We brought him home and dumped him out with the girls. Everyone was fine. No bouncing around or running away like horses, everyone was just fine. Strange. They stayed at Tom and Donna's until we finished the pasture fences. Steve and I had the bunkers finished, the fence was done, the gates were up and we had two low fifty gallon buckets for water. We had to run water from way up the hill because this was the only way to get water down there quickly. We had about four hundred feet of hose through the forest and down to the buckets. We had to turn on the water up top and then go down and open the nozzle to fill the tanks.

The day came and we loaded up the cattle through the chute and closed in all five head of cattle. We drove the five minutes to our house. We backed the trailer up to the gate and opened the door and out they went into this gorgeous forest with lots of grass. They bucked and kicked and had a great time running around. Oh boy, now we are responsible for them.

They were all very good. They learned the sound of the RTV and our call to "come cow" and they would come running to get their sunflower seeds and corn. Cattle are not friendly. They want to be fed and watered and left alone. I was in awe of them and very respectful of their power. Manly's neck filled the whole entrance to the feed bunker where they ate. When he wanted that spot, he just took it and no one messed with him. I saw him take down a four inch diameter tree just scratching his side. He was sheer power and a force to be reckoned with so I called him, fed him and left him alone. He was actually pretty quiet and did not cause a problem.

We realized that if we wanted to do anything with the cows in safety we would have to have a chute and a loading area and eventually a squeeze and a header. We decided it would cost too much to feed Manly over the winter and we were keeping Road Block and she would be too young to breed with so we had to sell Manly in August but we had to have a loading area because I was not standing out there with some panel hoping he would go where we wanted him to go.

Steve did the research and printed off about five copies of loading and working chutes. We picked one, bought the materials and got Josh to help us start building. I cannot believe every single one of those plans said the chute should not be wider than 30 inches, even for big cattle. I could not believe that and told Steve it was too narrow, they would get stuck but Steve did more research and that was the number. I thought we would have stuck cattle. Oh my. By this time we had moved the cattle to Cow 2 so we could work uninterrupted in cow 1. Steve and I had measured and flagged and planned and organized the whole working area. Josh is incredible. We used the tractor with the auger to dig the holes and we carried all this stuff down on the forks and Josh cleaned out all the holes by hand, put in a post and then tamped each one of these many rail road ties and posts into the ground. Steve and Josh cut the boards and put them up. It was not finished but it had a holding area, a crowding area, a divider gate for loading or letting cattle through and we had measured the truck and trailer area so it would all work.

Loading day came and Tom came over to help and Josh wanted to see how this awesome thing worked. Now, I am the big planner, organizer, decider who does what. We had the truck and trailer in place and I wanted to talk about who did what job and admire the whole thing. Tom walked in, pushed the cows into the crowding area and here they came. Holy crap. I am the only one standing near the separating gait. Here comes Midnight, she gets to go through move the gate, right behind her is Manly, quick switch the gate, with his nose on Manly's butt here is Delay. Manly gets diverted to the trailer, quick switch the gate so Delay goes through, and here comes White Face and Road Block and they have to go through. Who shuts the gate to the trailer before Manly comes back. Oh my gosh. Josh rushes over and shuts the trailer, I let White Face and Road Block through and the whole ordeal is over in fifteen seconds. I look at Tom and tell him I am not ready and he says you did great, it's done. I am whining about not knowing the jobs and we should talk about it and Tom says that all worked perfectly, you did a great job. I cannot believe it. It truly all went so fast and the whole chute worked exactly like it was supposed to work and none of the cattle got stuck. It seriously, all worked just perfectly; I just would have liked to talk about it a bit first. I guess that is why you do research and read—way to go Steve. He truly is amazing.

I think that both Tom and Josh and even Steve and I are all very pleased and impressed with how well the whole thing worked. Of course, had I not been quick with the gate it could have been a real bummer. I do not even want to think what would have happened if I had let the wrong cow in or if Manly had turned back around and come out. Thankfully, it all went well and we were proud and pleased.

I was not happy about selling Manly but I am enough of a mathematician to realize it would cost a lot and create a lot of problems to keep Manly so he had to be sold. We never saw him breed with either of the cows but since they both had calves he obviously did his job and both calves are big, strong, healthy and beautiful. Manly actually put on two pounds per day while he was at our house and he made us about $300 more than we bought him for so we were pleased.

Steve and I realized that we could not keep the cattle in the forest for the winter because that hose would freeze and we did not have time to dig the trench to get the water down there so we decided we would have to bring the cattle up where we could use a heated tank for water and had a frost free hydrant so we would not have to haul water but we would need a shelter. Road Block and Delay would have to be weaned so we needed to fix a separate area with electric fence so they could see their mom's but not get out. We had to build that fence but there was already a shelter there. Since we were using one of the horse areas for weaning we would need a new horse shelter and a new cattle shelter for winter.

So, this set into play a whole new series of building and a race against time before winter hit. We had to measure, plan, organize, and buy materials for both shelters. It was getting colder and we had to get these up. I told Steve we should put up the posts for the cattle shelter because if it froze we would never get them in the ground. We would be able to put up boards and tin if the posts were already up but we would not be able to dig in frozen ground. So, we did put up the posts. The very last post went into solid granite. The auger would not dig through that. Steve put up the other posts and I used a thirty-five pound digging bar made of steel with a hardened point to smash into the granite and then clear out the broken rock by hand. Yes, we are back to the free weight room stuff with all the reps with the digging bar. It took me several hours but by the time

Steve finished the other posts and had tamped them down, the hole in the granite was almost ready. Steve finished the last little bit and we got all the posts for the cattle shelter into the ground. We already had the horse shelter posts in the ground. It was a good thing because it froze that next week. We finally finished the horse shelter. The horse shelters take so long because all the wooden posts have to be covered with wire because the horses will chew the wood when they are bored so it takes forever. We did finish the horse shelter and did finish the cattle shelter just before November hit and we got the most snow ever recorded for November so it was good.

We had also been smart enough to bring up our early cured logs that were intended for fire wood. We knew we had to finish the shelters and did not have time to deal with this wood. So we brought it up to the end of the barn, stacked it and tarped it to keep it dry until we got to it. Another very smart decision on our part. We did get the wood cut, split and stacked so we had enough wood to burn all winter and the shelters were up so the animals had protection if they wanted it.

We were exhausted. It had taken us all summer with the help of Josh and Joe to build fenced cattle areas, cattle shelters, and weaning areas, fix the water area so both calves and cows could use the same heated tank, build a huge horse shelter, make a large caged area for chickens, build a fancy chicken house and get the wood ready for winter. Holy cow—what a busy summer!

Steve always does such a nice job. Our neighbors tease us about the "cow palace" and the "very fancy chicken house."

Chapter 18

WE HAVE BUFFALO

*H*oly cow. I had finished watching the eleven o'clock news and had just fallen asleep. Steve came in and woke me up saying there are huge animals out there. I looked out the window and he was right—it looked like a buffalo. I quickly got dressed—we don't go anywhere out here without getting completely dressed with boots and all because we do not know how long we will be out or what we will have to do.

As I slid on my muck boots I heard a thumping on the door and something very heavy walking across our wood patio. Oh boy, whatever it is it is coming inside. I got my down jacket and opened the door. It was our cows. Somehow they had gotten out. The steer was wandering over to the barn after trying the back door and walking on the patio. There were three sets of eyes at the end of the house—Midnight, White Face and Road Block. I am not sure what Steve was doing but I said I would get the RTV and some food. I always called them by saying "come cow" at meal times and they always came running to the RTV because that is what brought their food. I think basically I did not want to be walking around in the total dark with these huge animals and who knew where they would go—I wanted to be in my chariot—the RTV to protect me and help me run faster.

I got the RTV and got their orange bucket that I brought the grain with. I started up the RTV and started driving slowly up the hill to their pasture and calling "come cow, come cow" and shaking their grain bucket. Incredibly, as I drove up the hill all four of the cattle came running after me. Steve had the gate opened and took the bucket and shook it and started pouring it into their feeder while I closed the gate. They all happily walked in and ate their grain.

We decided that one of the cows had to be scratching their neck on the chain across the gate and with perfect timing must have sprung the latch and the gate was wide open so they just came out to explore. In the pitch black of night we figured they had only been out for a little while and we were so totally relieved that they had gone back in so easily. Ha—and the cowboys think this is so hard. Give me a break—we were very fortunate and again totally clueless. We went back to bed after double chaining the gate to the cattle area.

The next day when we got up we realized that they had been out for quite a while. It had been raining and the ground was still a little mucky so you could follow cow prints everywhere. Not only had they tested our house door but they had also been right up to the chicken coop door. In fact, they had walked through the extension cord that kept the heat lamp on in the chicken house and unplugged it. They had walked along all the buildings and wandered past the new building to where we had the round bales of alfalfa stored. You could see where they had stopped for a snack making big holes in the sides of the bales and leaving large cow patties. I mean seriously, these cows could have gone anywhere, down the road, into someone else's property. I mean heck, there are very few fences out here. They could have gone anywhere and caused all kinds of problems. Seriously, I think we were very fortunate or maybe it is just because we are such good providers or maybe they did not want to leave their water. I mean, who knows, the good news is that they stayed on the property and did not do too much damage and happily followed us back to their pasture. I wonder what the horses thought as these huge creatures meandered everywhere. It would have been interesting to have filmed the whole thing. Why do you think a cow would be pushing on doors and what if the back door had not been locked—do you think he might have come inside? What do you do with a thousand pound steer in the washroom and no room to turn around? I have not seen cows back up—now there is a thought.

Chapter 19

What was I thinking—Chickens

Holy cow. What was I thinking? We decided we were going to get chickens in the spring. I do not think we thought this whole thing through because we did not have a place to keep them but they were just small and we would work it out.

We went to our pet supply store and Steve started telling the lady what he wanted because he had already done the research and knew which breeds would do well in our climate. He said: "We want six of the Gold Sex Linked, six of the Buff Orpingtons" and then of course I was not interested in what he was saying. He had done the research and found that these were good laying chickens and also good to eat—I was not going to eat these chickens. I was standing there looking at this gorgeous, color poster of all these different kinds of chickens. They were beautiful, spectacular so I said "I want two of these and two of those and two of those." Steve said, "That is just too many chickens, what are you thinking." And I said "I think they are beautiful, and I want some of these." He let me have two of the Rhode Island Reds and only one of the Wyandotte's. I could not understand what the big deal was. When I was a kid we used to go to all the fairs at the local parks and they would have these games that if I could throw a ping pong ball into these little gold fish bowls I would get the gold fish and if I could throw the ring over the coke bottle then I could have a baby chicken. As kids we would go to these fairs and I would play all the games to win the fish and the chickens. I would bring them home and put the fish in a bowl and put chickens in a box and feed them bread crumbs and stuff and they would always die so I thought that half of the chickens we bought would die anyway so what did it matter how many we got. We ended up with fifteen and a little tray to feed chickens and a little water thing and of course real chick food—now there is a concept. We brought them home and got one of our big one hundred gallon horse tubs and put the chickens in it with their water and food tray. We had to put them in the tack room because it was still freezing out there and the tack room had a small heater that kept the room about fifty degrees. We also put in a heat lamp and got a big piece of spare chicken wire to put over the top.

We realized we needed to build a chicken yard and a chicken house. Since it was coming on spring we decided to build the chicken yard first. We made it twenty by twenty feet and put wire all around the sides and over the top because we have hawks, owls, falcons and eagles that are always hunting around our pastures. Steve made this cool door with a spring. He is so good at everything. It took us a couple weeks to do this because we sunk poles three feet in the ground, stapled everything and hooked the pieces of chicken wire together with j-clips every couple inches. I had done the math and figured out exactly how many rolls of wire and the right width of wire to avoid wasting anything, staples and etc. that we needed to complete the cage. My math really does come in handy. At this point the chickens were getting a bit big for the tub so we needed to get them into the day cage. Steve wanted to build a temporary box but I said that would take too long. I pointed out that if we used the bottom on the horse hay feeder and covered it with plywood that would work for a temporary home. Of course Steve made this perfect little house with a floor, to keep the chickens off the ground, darling little perches and a cute latch and a place to hang the water so they would not walk in it and a place to hang the heat lamp. Very impressive. We took their temporary tub and tipped it so the chickens could walk out into their new day area. They were darling. They had been in this small area so long that they all ran around together in that same size shape. We sat and laughed and watched them peck and explore and get more courageous. I think we watched them for an hour. It was delightful. We fixed a tarp so they would have shade in the hot sun or shelter from the rain.

At that point we started on the real chicken house. With Steve I do not know why I expected anything less than a perfect house. It turned out to be ten by twelve feet with windows on every side and painted soft yellow with white trim. All our farmer friends gave us a hard time about the Ritz Carlton for chickens—oh well. Half of Steve's enjoyment is the building. The inside has a divider with about eight feet wide for the chicken part and four feet for the people part. He again made this awesome, perfect door. He did the reading and research and figured out how high off the ground to make the nests, how many we needed and that they needed a little porch out in front of the nests. When we were building the floor I decided that I wanted vinyl on the floor so that it would be easy to clean, just sweep it out and spray it down if need be. I also suggested a sweep out door which Steve constructed. It has a removable section of the outside wall that is flush with the floor so I put the chickens in the day area and just sweep all the droppings and straw right out the door onto a tarp which can be dumped. It is incredible. It takes about ten minutes to sweep it all out. We have a college student that helps us with lots of things that we are getting too old to do. We had bought the vinyl on sale at a home improvement store for almost nothing because it had a few cuts in the edge which we would cover with walls anyway. It turns out his mom came home with that exact vinyl for the bathroom and he would not allow her to use it because it was chicken flooring. Way too funny.

I also came up with the idea that if we bought these cheap sink size plastic dish washing tubs and put them into the nests it would make them so much easier to clean. I come up with the ideas and Steve incorporates them. Anyway, we now have this Ritz Carlton of a chicken house that is insulated, painted yellow with white trim, has an old steel door that we had replaced from the house when we had the water heater problem, has a vinyl floor with sweep out, windows with Plexiglas for winter and removable pieces along the top edge to let in more air in the summer and keep out rain and cold in the winter and these way cool nests that are outside the cage with this lid that we lift and just reach in and pick up eggs. Just way too cool. This summer we will add an electric line so that we can have the heat lamp and something to keep the water from freezing. Because of our current configuration with the electric we could only have the heat lamp but we will fix that this summer.

Besides learning about chickens I also learned a lot about building the chicken house. I had seen our neighbor's chicken yard and the wire that they had over the day yard. That wire on top sagged really badly and I could not understand why unless they had not been careful putting it up or maybe some bird flew into it but I did not understand why it was sagging so badly. After our first snow I understood. Snow sits on top of chicken wire and builds up. It causes the whole top to sag and with enough weight could cause it to break or collapse. I found that if I took the pitch fork and pushed it up and bounced it that the snow would fall through. However, in order to do this I was almost standing right under the spot so of course I caused this huge mass of snow to fall on me. Since I had to do the entire twenty by twenty ceiling, that is four hundred square feet of snow that I dumped on myself but it needed to be done. I was a mess when I came back into the house and Steve asked what happened and I was slightly embarrassed but happy I had found the solution and would try to keep that ceiling from sagging.

You guessed it. All except one of our chickens is still alive and doing well. In the summer time we bring them greens from the garden and when they hear that gate open they all stand by the door and wait. They can strip a whole broccoli branch in about three minutes. They are so fun to watch and they are beautiful. We have one rooster in the group. He is twice as big as all the chickens and his name is Godzilla. He is spectacular but has no social graces. He grabs these girls by the back of the head, walks on them and when he is finished walks on their head as he leaves. He is, however, a good leader. Whenever we bring out food he makes these great sounds and tells his flock that food is here. We also have No Butt, one of the Rhode Island reds because she just has a smooth butt with no tail feathers that stick up like the other chickens. We also have Gimp because something happened to her leg and she limps but she is a survivor. My favorite color is Spice. She is a black and white Wyandotte kind of like salt and pepper and just really pretty. The Buff Orpingtons jump any time you come in with food, they are too fun.

Oh my, they started laying eggs—big beautiful, brown eggs and they are good. However, we get about a dozen every day. Now, it is tough for two people and five Labrador retrievers to keep up with that many eggs. I started baking and made chocolate chip cookies that take four eggs and then brownies that took two eggs and then we had some double yoked eggs. Now, does that count as one egg or two? I have no idea. I gave two eggs a day to each dog which made some horrendous gas and after a while even the dogs got tired of that many eggs. I gave some to friends, I sold some to friends, and we hard boiled them and fed them back to the chickens. I found that with about a dozen a day it does not take too many days to fill a refrigerator. What was I thinking—all but one of the chickens lived and they all lay eggs except Godzilla. We have learned to cook a few more meals that use eggs and I give some to friends that sell them and the dogs still get some and we are finding a happy medium.

We love the chickens and find great joy in them and they are beautiful, fun to watch and the eggs are great. We are not eating these chickens like some people think we should—they are part of the family.

Chapter 20

THE CHICKEN ATTACK

*I*t was a gorgeous day. It was one of the first days of spring that actually had full sun. The day before we had one inch of snow and because the temperature got down to 27 degrees that night the new snow stuck around until about ten the next morning when it finally melted off.

Out here in the country people help each other all the time. It is a refreshing exchange of kindness and also a necessity at times.

At any rate, our neighbors who own cattle had been keeping our new bull for us through the winter. We had both bought new bulls from a friend of his so Tom and Donna had offered to keep our bull so they would both have company and because we did not have a safe spot for a bull yet. So, to help defray some of the cost of feeding him I would bring her eggs that she would sell along with her eggs to a growing clientele. We were getting about a dozen eggs per day so about once a week I would bring her all the eggs we had not needed.

I usually take care of the horses, cattle, cat, dogs and Steve takes care of the chickens and also fixes all the things I break or need help with.

We had just taken three dozen eggs to our friend and she called and said they had sold them all and had people coming the next day to get more so I told her I would bring what I had in the morning after I finished the chores. I had just finished feeding all the animals and decided to get today's eggs because we only had two dozen and needed a few more to fill out the third dozen. Steve happened to walk up at that time. I had just opened the hinged door that covers the nests so I can stand outside and get eggs without having to go into the cage. I noticed that there was only one egg and a chicken sitting on the end nest. The chickens like that end nest box the best and will frequently have five or six eggs in there. I asked Steve if I should move her over to get the egg and he said sure because we needed three more to fill out that last dozen. I picked up an egg box and held it by the end and then placed the single egg at the far end of the box. I then stuck my hand under the chicken and she pecked me—yikes, where did that come from. I looked in the box and the one egg I had was gone. Steve was standing behind me in absolute hysterics because when I jumped I obviously catapulted that one egg into the air and it smashed on the floor. I looked at it, looked at the chicken, and could not believe Steve was laughing so hard and decided that I was not quite the farmer I thought I had become. Being the knight in shining armor, Steve took the box, lifted the chicken and grabbed two eggs. He had the gall to tell me that we would have had three had I not flung the other egg. We both stood there and laughed and said we would get one from our refrigerator from the one dozen we had kept for ourselves. We dragged the door mat out, washed the squashed egg off of it and set it out to dry.

We then took the full three dozen to our friends so she could sell them. I told her my story and she also laughed and said that her kids did not like to get the eggs because chickens do peck. She also discussed several ways that worked to get eggs from under a sitting chicken. Obviously, I still have a lot to learn.

Chapter 21

THE GIANT COW PATTY

*I*t was cold and snowing but the cattle needed more food. We had bought these big, round alfalfa bales that weighed about 700 pounds each. Everyone just stores them out in the open so the rain and snow fall on them. They are made by rolling up the alfalfa cuttings until it gets big enough to tie with twine. We have to move them with a special tool on the tractor because they are too big to move them any other way. Because of the rain and snow the outside layers get wet and sometimes a little moldy. The cattle can eat that without a problem but it is not good for the horses. The bales have a diameter of about four to five feet so we would take the outside foot of wet alfalfa and peel it off in the cattle pen and then take the rest into the barn and peel it off for horses or cattle but all the wet stuff had to be peeled off and the cattle loved it. We had to peel it off in the cattle pen because once it was peeled off it was very difficult and awkward to move it anywhere else.

The ground was frozen hard and the cow patties were everywhere. There was hay tromped into the ground and the ground was very uneven. Because the cows would stand right there and try to eat the alfalfa as Steve peeled it off the bale while the tractor held the bale in the air I was out there with my sorting stick to keep them out of his way. Seriously, I was such a big threat to hungry cows standing there brandishing my stick. Anyway, Steve was driving the tractor up to the designated spot and I was walking along beside the tractor and watching the cows to keep them out of the way. I was not watching the ground. I hit this 20 pound—no kidding—massive, frozen mound of cow poop and went flat on my face in all this gunk. Actually, I was pretty proud of myself because I was strong enough and quick enough to land in the push up position while keeping my face from being embedded in another cow patty. Steve stopped the tractor and started looking for me only to find me in the gunk. He started laughing and asked what happened because I had just disappeared from sight. Of course I was embarrassed and quite dirty but except for my ego I was basically unhurt. He peeled off the hay and I poked at the cows and we got out of there. Who would have thought cows could make a huge pile like that—it was impressive and totally frozen solid—of course, maybe that was better than fresh. I guess it could have been worse.

Chapter 22

THE HAWK

We had not been at the ranch for very long. I was out raking up old hay with my constant companions—Rocky, Magic, Jake and Lucky, our Labrador retrievers. They were running around smelling everything, marking everything and digging for gophers. I took a break and leaned on my rake to watch at the exact moment that a small rodent popped out of a hole and took off running. Jake saw him at the same time and took off after him. Just as Jake was about to pounce on this rodent from out of the sky came this incredible hawk that swooped down and grabbed this small animal and took off with it dangling from his talons. Jake got there and leaped only to have his jaws snap shut on nothing. We all stood there and watched in total awe. Wow, I felt like I was in some nature show or something. I mean, how many people get to watch nature at work right in their back yard. I was impressed, Jake could not believe it and the hawk flew off with dinner and I was pleased to have one less gopher.

Chapter 23

LICORICE—THE NEW BABY CALF

White Face had not yet delivered her calf. We had been watching her carefully for weeks and knew that she was close. Her udder was so big I was sure if you touched it that it would just pop. We had gone to town the week before and run several errands including a stop at Costco. When we got back Midnight had already delivered her new baby calf by herself and we named her Costco. She was pure black, big, strong, wobbly but beautiful.

I had checked White Face at l: 30 in the afternoon and she was fine. I went back up at 2:30 and she had her butt mashed up against the barbed wire fence. This was definitely not normal and I was afraid she was going to hurt herself—if nothing else, I thought she might pop that udder. I went to get Steve and we went back to check her out. Steve walked along the fence line and pushed her off the fence. Oh Boy, she had a foot sticking out—the baby was coming. I ran down the hill and called our cattle friends, Tom and Donna. They had been in the cattle business for 30+ years and had seen it all. Donna told me that if I went back up the hill and the baby was not born she was in trouble and I should come to get them. I went back up the hill and there was no baby—just a foot. I got into the truck and drove to our friend's place that was 5 minutes away. I said, there is no baby yet and the foot is sticking out and can you help us. I am sure I was just a little hysterical but they did not seem to notice. Donna was trying to get dinner on and I wanted them to stop everything and come help but I was trying to be calm—not. Tom grabbed a chain and some metal handles and they told me to go get the calf puller. Oh my, what does a calf puller look like—well we had seen one on a show Steve was watching so I looked for it and found one. They said it was the wrong one and grabbed the right one. I drove them back. We had gotten caught short that winter and had not finished all our cattle area. We had barely finished the new cattle shelter and felt very fortunate. We had put in the posts before the ground froze and had finished the shelter just as winter hit hard and we were happy to have shelter for our pregnant cows. At any rate, we had not built the catching area. What does that mean—; we had to chase these cows to catch White Face. Midnight had her less than a week old Costco and all three of them ran around together. We brought in portable steel panels that we had for the horses and kind of closed off part of the shelter and fixed a panel so we could squeeze White Face up against a wall. Cattle are powerful and can kill you if they feel threatened. We used the RTV to try to herd these cattle down to the paneled area. Poor little Costco was exhausted. I think that White Face really knew we wanted to help her. After about 15 minutes we finally got them down to the right area. Midnight went into the shelter but came out and Costco stayed in and White Face stayed in. The first thing we had to do was get Costco out so Midnight would not be a problem. We got Costco out, she was so tired, her little tongue was hanging out—not good but she went to lie down and Midnight stayed there to protect her. Steve used one of the panels to squeeze White Face into the corner. We used the RTV to support the front panel. White Face was squeezed in with her face back in the corner and her butt facing out. Tom took the chain and wrapped it around one foot, found the other foot and wrapped it also. He hooked the two handles onto the chain and pulled—nothing. Steve who was holding the squeeze panel and Donna on the other side both massaged the skin around her labia to help peel it back. White Face pushed and Tom pulled—here comes the nose and a purple tongue. Another squeeze and another pull and the head is out. Several more pushes by White Face and a lot of pulling by Tom and the baby comes out and plops on the ground. Tom quickly uses straw to help clear its nose. It is breathing. White Face wants her baby. Everyone gets out and Steve ties the panels in place so we can keep them in the shelter over night. White Face starts to lick her baby. She has all this after birth stuff hanging out—yuk, but that is normal. Tom says "Wow, that is a huge calf, no wonder she was having trouble."

Of course, I am clueless and have no idea if this is a big calf or not. I can see that it is alive and I am pleased. White Face licks her baby and he starts to move a little more. Tom and Donna gather their stuff and get ready to go home. "Hey, wait, aren't we supposed to watch and do more stuff." Tom and Donna have their own chores to do and saving our cow and calf is just part of their day. Holy cow. I am shaking. The adrenaline is pumping and I am kind of trying to decide what to do next. Nothing. I was pleased we had not had to use the calf puller. It is a steel contraption that has a bar that goes against the cows back legs and butt and then you hook the chain to the ratchet and you crank. I guess pulling calves is not a strange thing to cattle people. If you do not get to the cow soon enough the cow can die, the baby can die or they can both die so if that baby is too big, which he was, they need help. It was so fortunate that this went on in the middle of the day because she would have gotten weaker as the night went on and she could not have pushed him out. I learn again that I am not prepared. We will have the chain, handles and calf puller thing before next calf season.

We go back up to check on White Face and she has licked her baby dry and it is trying to get up. He gets up and wobbles and tries to nurse. He is not sure and fumbles around but he is up and he is looking. We watch until he finally finds a teat and begins to nurse. White Face still has the afterbirth hanging out. Oh dear, if it does not come out it could be another possible problem. We leave them and come back to check later. Oh yeah, the afterbirth came out and she is eating it—oh gross. I guess they do that so the blood does not attract predators—coyotes, we have a lot of those. We are leaving them in the shelter for the night so we can give a shot, tag and band this new baby the next day. The new baby's name is Licorice. He is a solid black, pure Black Angus little guy and he is darling.

The next day Tom and Donna come back and we catch Licorice and use a panel to keep White Face separate. She is actually pretty good. I think she knows that we helped her and feels safe with us but we still respect her space as cattle can be unpredictable. Tom catches Licorice, snaps the ear tag that we have ready into his ear, gives him the shot of selenium called BoSe and then uses this strange little gadget that holds a small rubber band wide open and you put the testicles into it and then let go. The rubber band squeezes enough that it cuts off the blood supply to the testicles and they dry up and drop off—oh gag me. However, this is much more humane than cutting them off when they are older and risk infection and all kinds of problems. I am not happy about this but cattle are not pets and we have a new young bull that will breed this spring.

The idea is that each spring the cows breed with the bull and each year there are more calves. The idea is not to have open cows, that is cows that are not pregnant because it is too expensive to feed open cows through winter.

We will keep White Face, Midnight, Costco and Road Block who is the yearling calf of White Face from last year. So this year we will have three cows to breed and should have three new babies next year.

Wow, we have learned so much and are so indebted to our cattle friends Tom and Donna. We brought them pizza, salad and homemade chocolate chip cookies for dinner and they said we did not have to do that. Are you kidding—that whole scenario was amazing and I was totally unprepared for any of it. I mean seriously, people take classes and stuff to learn about things like that and these people just treat it like part of a normal day.

Again, I am humbled by the whole series of events. I cannot believe how much I learn every single day. This farming life is tough and we are just doing it on a very small scale.

Chapter 24

HE'S OUT

*I*had gone out to feed the morning breakfast and I could not find the cattle. I drove back to the back and found Midnight and her new calf Costco and White Face, the new mom for two days, but her baby, Licorice, was on the wrong side of the fence. Licorice was only two days old and we have coyotes. I was immediately thankful that he was alive and was impressed that the rest of the cows just waited quietly by the new calf. We had company and I knew I was not capable of catching this calf myself. I drove back down the hill to get Steve and Donald, one of our guests who was just getting up. Steve was still asleep. I woke him up and told him Licorice was out. We knew this could be a problem because Licorice liked to sleep in the small rain gulley and the fence was a little higher there. We felt it was possible that he could wake up and get up on the wrong side of the fence which is what we think happened. We had talked about it but thought—what are the chances in the first couple days—obviously 100% chance since he was out.

Steve got up and Donald came to help. We drove back to the back to analyze the situation. The cows were now up and patiently waiting but obviously concerned about Licorice as they waited for us to fix this problem. Even very young calves are strong, can run fast for short distances and can kick the heck out of you. Plus the fact that who knew what mom on the other side of the fence might do so we knew we needed to be careful. We had divided this pasture in half with a barbed wire fence. Donald walked down the middle fence, I walked up that side fence and Steve came from the middle so we kind of cornered him with the fences. Steve is a master at anything and we had the big railroad ties with cross pieces in the corner. It was a little higher there so the plan was to catch Licorice and shove him back under that wire. We all walked slowly and herded Licorice back toward that corner where both moms were now anxiously hanging out on the other side of that fence. Steve threw an arm over Licorice and kind of grabbed him. I was surprised that this two day old calf could cause Steve any trouble. Steve pushed him on his butt to stop those legs from kicking and pushed his head down under that bottom wire and then Steve and Donald pushed him across under the wire where the moms seemed quite relieved and took the unhurt Licorice and Costco away from us—basically indignant but I think relieved to have Licorice back. Both Midnight and White Face are very good moms and basically I think they trust us to feed and take care of them but there is no doubt in my mind that if they wanted to or even decided to they could easily hurt us so we are always very respectful of their abilities.

Donald, a paramedic in San Diego, laughed and said "I do not know what I would have done had he come my way—I guess tackle him." Now there is a thought. Heck, there is no way my old body could have done anything had he come my way—these old bones don't move like they used to be able to move. I had not even considered what I would do except flap my arms, run two steps at him and try to persuade him that I was scary so he would go the other way. Good thing I had not thought about it.

Donald and I came back later with a section of small square wire mesh and used bale twine to tie it to the barbed wire and kind of close off that one little spot. Licorice has not been out since then and I have seen him sleeping in that same spot.

Chapter 25

I Thought He Was Dead

*I*t was a cool, overcast day. I had done all my chores and finally had a chance to take Rudy for a ride. The four chocolate labs came with me. I rode the fence line just to see what damage the deer had done to it during the winter. It was crisp and cool and oh so beautiful out. As I came to the top of the hill by our little tree forest Shadow went over to look at a pile of bird feathers. I thought some bird had been eaten. As I came closer I saw that it was a young eagle lying on his back and he was looking at me. I called Shadow and told him to get away which he did very quickly because as I discovered later the eagle had either bitten or clawed his ear—not a bad wound but enough to know not to mess with the bird. The eagle was still alive. I rode back to put the dogs away and get Steve to see if we could help. I thought maybe the eagle had been shot or broken a wing or something. I got Steve and we drove back up in the RTV. I brought an old towel so we could wrap him up if we needed to do that.

When we got to the eagle he was definitely still alive and laying on his back in a depression in the ground and under the wire fence. We could not see any blood and he tried to flap his wings which just brushed the dirt up and down since he was on his back. His head and eyes followed us. He looked fierce but yet definitely in trouble. I wanted to wrap him in the towel but Steve said no way was he getting that close because the beak and talons could do major damage. Steve got our smooth cattle stick and walked over to him. He touched the talons on his left foot and pulled, the eagle lost his grip. Steve touched the talons again and this time he grabbed it and held on to the stick as if he knew we were trying to help. Steve pulled slowly and the eagle held on until he was on his stomach. The eagle's grip was so tight that Steve had to use his foot to help slide the talons off the pole. The eagle stood there and we waited. He was mottled brown with baby feather fuzz so we thought he was young. After a couple minutes he stretched out his wings and flew, he hit the fence, hit the tree and hit the other fence. My heart ached. I so wanted him to be safe. We knew that he was not injured if he could fly but he was so young he was not very good at flying yet. He dropped down to the ground and just stood there. We debated as to whether or not we should get him and put him in a tree but decided that we had given him a chance and would let him rest where he was. We started to drive back down the hill and were checking out the horse corridor for our rotational grazing system. The grass was not up yet and we had not had a chance to take down the electric system before winter caught us this year so we decided to check it out. As we went down the hill we heard this big whoosh, whoosh and saw a huge brown eagle fly by and it was oh so low and close. It bounced off a tree, went to another tree and then finally settled in the third tree. I told Steve that was our eagle and he said he did not think so but we drove back up to check and our eagle was gone. So, our young eagle did get up and did fly and hopefully is still safe out there.

Chapter 26

BUCK AND THE MARIGOLDS

*I*t was a cool spring day and the grass around the house and barn was tall, green and gorgeous. I turn the big geldings out to graze and they do a wonderful job of mowing, edging and fertilizing. They really do a good job on the hills and hard places to get close to with the mower. It also saves the pastures and lets them grow a little longer before I turn the horses out there. I used to make a big deal and spend hours setting up our portable fences and keeping them in a specific area. It would take the horses one day of grazing to eat that area. I finally evolved into closing the driveway that leads to the road, putting a gate across the barn and closing off the road that goes to the other side of the barn. I just open the gate to their normal loafing area and out they come. They eat everything and clean it all down. They are especially good at edging around the buildings, logs, planters and trees. They are amazing.

We have a wooden porch around our house and I was worried that they would tramp on that but since there is so much grass everywhere else they just stay off the porch. I do, however, have a few planters on the edge of the porch. My brother Lad has planted these planters with all kinds of gorgeous flowers but the flowers die each winter and the deer eat the plants when they finally start to bloom so basically I put about ten dollars of marigolds in the different planters and then plant marigold seeds next to the plants and the deer do not bother them, the horses do not like them and I have gorgeous color all summer long for very little money.

I never do understand why with all that good grass that they check out the trash cans. They knock the lids off and sniff around to see if there is anything good. They also dump them over which totally annoys me. Of course, it might be because we keep all the grains and stuff in trash cans in the barn and they know that.

When I have the horses out grazing around the house I usually work in the house so I can keep an eye on them. Our house has windows everywhere and I so love looking out the windows and watching these beautiful creatures as they edge right around the base of the house.

Buck is so smart, has no fears and does exactly what he wants to do. I happened to look out the window and there was Buck with his muzzle in my marigold planter. He was not eating the plants but nuzzling the dirt—for what I have no idea but he seemed to be fascinated with it. I did not want him to wreck my marigolds so I grabbed the closest thing which was a plastic bag—duh—Buck is not afraid of much. I walked up to him and flapped it in his face and he looked at me—like what the heck. I only had my house slippers on and did not want to get on the wet grass so I flapped it at him a bit more and pushed him away. I walked back into the house and looked out the window and he was back in the marigolds. I grabbed a broom—thought I could reach him better. Buck seemed to be enjoying the game. I shook it at him, plopped it on his shoulder and he took two steps away. I showed him. I walked back into the house and looked out the window and the beast was back in the planter. I grabbed the umbrella and popped it open at him a few times. He just looked at me. I went back into the house and he was back in the planter so I put my boots on, grabbed the broom, walked in the wet grass and finally chased him off. By that time I was giggling hysterically and enjoyed the game almost as much as Buck had enjoyed it. Each time he would pretend to eat grass until I got into the house and he was back at the marigolds. Buck had figured out the game.

The next day he was at it again but Steve saw him and Steve was dressed with boots and ready for the day. Steve grabbed the broom and walked right out there and chased Buck off. Too bad, Buck is very respectful of Steve and recognizes him as the real herd leader.

Chapter 27

RUDY THINKS HE'S SPECIAL

*R*udy is special and gets special treatment. He is the horse I ride almost every day even if it is for just half an hour when we are busy. I can get his feet cleaned, brushed and tacked up and ready to go in ten minutes. Rudy will go anywhere, anytime and do anything I ask him to do. He is a delight to ride and work with. Rudy is a very hard keeper. He has always been that way. Each day I bring him down and give him grains, equine senior and extra alfalfa. He likes being by himself and will kick the wall if I put a horse next to him. He definitely thinks he is special. Sometimes, I fix up Rudy's extra food, walk up the hill, open the gate to just let him out and he jogs down to his stall in the barn and happily starts eating his goodies. If I am late to bring him down he will pace at the fence and stare at me until I feel guilty and bring him down. I know he is spoiled but it is tough not to spoil him when he is such a wonderful horse to ride and work with.

I had let all the geldings out to graze on the rich, green grass around the house. It was cool and had just rained and they were all feeling good. Rudy took off first and ran down to the barn to see if his special food was there but I had closed off the barn. The rest of the geldings followed him down and Rudy obviously felt they were in his space and he reared up on his hind feet and then bucked and kicked and just threw this temper tantrum. The other geldings just bucked and ran around and played the game. They finally all settled down, found their favorite spot to graze and ignored me.

When I was convinced there would not be a problem I walked over to the house. Rudy bolted over to within ten feet in front of me and reared up, bucked, kicked and pranced around as if to tell me he needed his special food right now. I watched him, talked to him and walked into the house. He did settle down and grazed happily for an hour and then I took him in for his special stuff. I thought he was pretty funny.

About the Author

Jo Ann Byars earned her BA and MA from Long Beach State University in Southern California. She taught high school physical education, English, math and coached boys' and girls' volleyball and boys' and girls' swimming for thirty-four years. She spent three years in Hawaii when her husband was stationed at Kaneohe. During that time she taught math and coached girls' volleyball for Punahou private school for a year and a half. Jo has always been an avid athlete and outdoor enthusiast. She competed in volleyball, swimming, basketball, field hockey and softball. While in Hawaii she was certified to scuba dive and she and her husband loved to kayak. She and her brother used to play beach volleyball in Newport Beach, ride roller skates and bikes. Since Jo and her husband Steve have retired she swims and spends her days riding horses and working on projects at their ranch.

www.ingramcontent.com/pod-product-compliance
Lightning Source LLC
Chambersburg PA
CBHW020245290526
45784CB00003B/1103